I SHOULDA SAID . . .

A Treasury of Insults, Put-Downs, Boasts, Praises, Witticisms, Wisecracks, Comebacks and Ad-Libs

William H. Roylance

PARKER PUBLISHING COMPANY, INC

West Nyack, N.Y.

© 1973 by

Parker Publishing Company, Inc.

West Nyack, N.Y.

Library of Congress Cataloging in Publication Data

Roylance, William H
    I shoulda said ...

    1. American wit and humor.   I. Title.
PN6162.R67   73-5562

Printed in the United States of America.

A Word From The Author

This is not just another joke book. Great care was taken to make sure that it not be so. It was designed to give the maximum readability, pleasure and usefulness to every public speaker and every other person who speaks, whether he is most articulate or one who lets a choice wisecrack elude him until he can only mourn, "I shoulda said!" Now, swiftly, before you write off my comments to turgid hyperbole, I shall give you proof by listing the many unique and valuable features which this book contains:

MEMORY-MAKERS! How useless is the joke that can't be remembered! There are no such forget-them-as-fast-as-you-read-them witticisms in this volume. Each laugh-getter has a mental "hook" to place it indelibly in your mind for instant delivery to your tongue. This memory fastener consists of a short title description of the joke. By simply remembering the one- or two-word title you will have a reminder for the complete wisecrack.

Experienced speakers customarily make notes for their speeches by jotting down a short series of reminders. But this is perhaps the first book to have such built-in memory fixers. If you should find remembering even the short titles too taxing, then you simply need write them in your speech notes or on a palm-sized "crib" card for parties and private get-togethers, where a quick glance will jog your memory for a quick run to laughter.

A COMPREHENSIVE CROSS-INDEX! How useless is the wisecrack that can't be found! True, most joke books contain a table of contents in the front of the book. If this does not have the subject you have in mind under a certain word, you either have to look through the entire book, or try to think of other subjects it might be under, or be left jokeless.

Each section of this book is preceded by a short list of contents. However, these lists are supplemented in the back of the book by a complete cross-index. Here, by looking for any desired subject under almost any word, you will be led to every reference pertaining to it. Where there may be a long list of references for a particular subject, these will be found under a main heading to which related headings refer. For example, if you are interested in a bit of humor about people's looks, you will find in the index: "Looks — see Personal Appearance for cross-reference." Then under "Personal Appearance" you will find a lengthy list of cross-reference subjects related to this topic.

Most subjects are followed by numbers. These numbers refer not to pages but rather to the numbers accompanying all of the jokes in the book, and this joke numbering system is another valuable feature of this volume. It permits the index to lead you to the exact items you need rapidly, rather than giving you the number of a page that may contain much superfluous material. This system further permits you to place the number of the joke alongside the title when you place it in your speech notes or "crib" card. Then, if you should have need to look up that joke again, you can find it immediately from its number.

A COMPREHENSIVE CROSS-SECTION OF HUMOR AND WIT! How limited is the book that's confined to a few types of humor such as aphorisms or stories! The very title of this volume tells you how comprehensive is its material. Part I contains a large selection of ever-enjoyable insults and put-downs. Part II contains the more uncommonly found but uncommonly useful boasts and praises. (A witty or humorous boast or praise can win enemies or friends respectively and respectfully.) Part III offers a treasure of universally popular witticisms, wisecracks, comebacks and "ad-libs." Combined, the three parts give a tremendous variety of more than 2,000 separate items, any combination of which is sure to make any speech a success.

FRESH, ORIGINAL, AND BRIEF LAUGHMAKERS! How valueless is the book replete with wordy and stale stories! Many of these are mere corncribs — repositories for stolen and abominable jokes. Who has the time or desire to meander through endless maunderings? The essence of both wit and good humor is brevity. So this volume is confined to fresh and original *material only*. It has the quickest and most delightful of quips — short, lean, hit-em-hard, one-and-not-much-more liners. And for the ultimate in brevity it even includes a few one-worders under Epithets in Part I.

READABILITY! How limited is the worth of a book which may have some value as a reference work for jokes but is unreadable for enjoyment because of its arid expanses of sameness! It is pleasant to just sit down and read this book, partly because of its variety and division into parts. But more importantly, this book has an added feature not to be found in any other. At the end of many sections is a subdivision of "Suppose that" situations which place you in funny yet fairly common situations that cry out for a humorous response. These make for enjoyable reading but also suggest many occasions for which the book's material can be used.

SPECIAL JOKES FOR SPECIAL SPEECHES! How confining and ordinary is the book which makes you figure out and then ferret out the appropriate jokes for a particular type of speech! Perhaps the most valuable and original feature of this volume is one that precludes the necessity for such an onerous chore. This is Part IV, "Lines for Special Occasions," where a table of contents lists dozens of special meetings, parties, rallies, conventions, dinners, etc. at which you may have been invited to offer some choice words. After you have looked up the page number for your "special occasion," there you will find a series of guffaw-getters and mirth-shakers designed for just such an occasion. Think of the advantages of just looking up the occasion rather than the jokes!

There you have them — the features that make this the most unusual and profitable book of its type. They make it one that is long overdue from the publishers (and, I suspect, at the libraries as well). It is your hilarium of boppers, whoppers and stoppers, all of them toppers. Enjoy and employ this book and you will find that not only will you need never again say "I shoulda said," but that your listeners will say "I wish *I'd* said that!"

William H. Roylance

By the Same Author:

Complete Book of Insults, Boasts, and Riddles

Contents

Part I Insults and Putdowns

Part I Insults and Putdowns (cont.)

Part II Boasts and Praises

Part II Boasts and Praises (cont.)

Part III Witticisms, Wisecracks and Comebacks

Part III Witticisms, Wisecracks and Comebacks (cont.)

Part IV Ad Libs and Lines for Special Occasions

Part IV Ad Libs and Lines for Special Occasions (cont.)

Part IV Ad Libs and Lines for Special Occasions (cont.)

Part V   Cross Reference Index

Part I
Insults and Putdowns

Abasements
Actress
Ancestors
Attire
Baby
Banker
Beard
Birth
Bore
Brain
Candy
Charm
Congratulations
Crabbiness
Death Wish
Dishonesty
Dizziness
Doctors
Drinking
Epithets
Evil
Face
Failures
Family
Fatness
Females
Figure
Filth

Food
Forgetfulness
Friends
Garbage
Genocide
Gold Diggers
Gossip
Hair
Hard Up
Hate
Heads
Health Nuts
Heart
Hell
Henpecked
Homeliness
Humor
Illiteracy
Immorality
Imprisonment
Inferiority
Insanity
Insults
Jabs
Job
Killing
Lateness
Lawyer

Laziness
Lies
Lipstick
Logic
Looks
Mate
Mind
Mistakes
Mouth
Nag
Nightmares
Old Fashioned
Oldness
Opinionated
Pain
Pennypinching
Personality
Pretense
Repulsiveness
Reputation

Retorts
Self Love
Selfishness
Skin
Smoking
Sourness
Speaking — Speech
Specimen
States
Stupidity
Talking
Tearfulness
Thinking
Tolerance
Unfaithfulness
Violence
Waiter
Weakness
Wit
Writing

ABASEMENTS

Suppose that someone has just said or done something to hurt your feelings. You wish to retaliate by humbling and humiliating him. Then use one or more of the following:

Company*

1 I'm looking forward to the pleasure of your company, since I haven't enjoyed it yet.

Look ma

2 What's that statement supposed to be saying — "Look ma, no brains"?

Introduce to friends

3 I'd like to introduce you to some friends of mine. I want to break off with them.

Comes to mouth

4 You have the habit of saying the first thing that comes to your mouth.

Capital case

5 Murdering you would be a capital case. Just capital.

Great pains

6 I'd go to great pains to not know you. I've certainly suffered them by knowing you.

Cause of death

7 When you pass away and somebody asks the cause of death, I'll say your stupidity.

Caterpillar

8 You're metamorphosing into a caterpillar.

Dreams

9 Goodbye! I'll see you in my dreams — if I eat too much.

Abject lesson

10 I've learned a lot from you. You're an abject lesson.

Infatuation

11 I've had many cases of love that were just infatuation, but this hatred I feel for you is the real thing.

*This word is the mental hook which will help you remember the line.

Best at all you do
12 You're the best at all you do — and all you do is make people hate you.

Working hard
13 Don't you realize there are enough people to hate in the world already without your working so hard to give us another?

Forgetting oneself
14 In your case it's being selfish to forget yourself.

Admiration
15 I must have a deep admiration for you. It's so deep it's not visible.

Attention
16 When you start talking I pay attention — to make sure I don't hear anything you say.

Garbage disposal unit
17 I'd like to try out my new garbage disposal unit. Why don't you go jump from a 50-story building and I'll pour you into it.

Loathe as much
18 The thing that terrifies me the most is that someone might hate me as much as I loathe you.

Accident
19 When you get run over by a car it shouldn't be listed under accidents.

ACTRESS
Suppose that an obnoxious actress at a cocktail party has bent your ear in boasting. You gain revenge:

Willing to act
20 The trouble with both the world and your theater is that people aren't willing to act.

Thunderous reception
21 I've noticed the thunderous reception when you appear. The audience sounds like a stampede as it leaves the theater.

Sensitive performance
22 Yes, you've given many sensitive performances. In fact, you're as touchy as a land mine.

Entertain doubt

23 You couldn't even entertain a doubt.

ANCESTORS

Millions of ancestors

24 All of your ancestors must number into the millions. It's hard to believe that many people are to blame for producing you.

Traced ancestry

25 He traced his ancestry until he became horrified by the picture it was forming.

Family tree

26 Ever since I saw you on your family tree I've wanted to cut it down.

Mayflower

27 I hear your ancestors came over on the Mayflower. Did they walk up the hawser?

ATTIRE

Too short

28 Your dress is too short. It only extends up to your neck.

Cowhide

29 Where did you get that beautiful cowhide you're wearing? Does it look as good on you when you're undressed?

New tie

30 I really like to wear this tie you gave me. You have to look at it; I don't.

New shirt

31 New shirt? Or is that a new strain of gravy?

Museum

32 Your clothes don't belong in a closet. They belong in a museum.

Current style

33 That dress must be the current style. It gives people a jolt.

Ragpicker

34 When did you become a ragpicker?

Tear off

35 Men want to tear off your clothes — they're so ugly.

Kept up

36 Your clothes are always neat and well kept. Too bad — if they weren't, you'd buy some new ones.

Shroud

37 Of your loud apparel be not proud. . . If there were justice they'd be your shroud.

Colors

38 Her clothes always are of a color to please everyone. The trouble is, they include all the repulsive colors as well.

Dirty looks

39 With her clothes she never elicits dirty thoughts from men — only dirty looks.

Wig

40 I hope that's a wig you're wearing. I wouldn't want to think it's real.

Shake head

41 I used to shake my head at the sight of your clothes. Now my whole body shudders.

Ugly on you

42 Are those clothes really as ugly as they look or is it just because they're on you?

Clothes become you

43 You've certainly made those clothes become you. In fact they're so ugly they must have become you.

Medal

44 He got a medal for bravery — for appearing in those clothes.

Style setter

45 She's a style setter. When she wears a style, it sets.

Sets sex back

46 That dress just set sex back 100 years.

Latest styles

47 She always wears the latest styles. In fact, they're always too late.

Low cut

48 That dress is cut so low she looks as though she's going to her coming-out party.

Ragtime

49 The only music to play with those clothes is ragtime.

BABY

Mafia

50 When he was a child, his mother tried to hire someone to take care of him. But the Mafia wanted too much.

BANKER

Needy

51 A banker is one of the few businessmen who doesn't profit from the needy — because he won't lend money to anyone who needs it.

BEARD

Stubble bum

52 Why don't you shave, you stubble bum?

Grew on you

53 That beard may have grown on you, but it's too ugly to grow on anyone else.

BIRTH

Suppose that you wish to decelebrate somebody's birthday:

Laid egg

54 Are you the result of a viviparous birth or were you born because someone laid an egg?

Denial

55 He's so homely that not only did his father deny his paternity, his mother denied he was her son while watching him being born.

Police station

56 I hear that when your mother first saw you she decided to leave you on the front steps of a police station while she turned herself in.

Infanticide

57 He was born because his mother didn't believe in abortion. Now she believes in infanticide.

Accident of birth

58 No one should be punished for accident of birth, but you look too much like a wreck not to be.

Unnatural birth

59 His was an unnatural birth. He came from a human being.

Answer to prayer

60 He was the answer to prayer. His parents prayed that the world be made to suffer and here he came.

BORE

Kick habit

61 You're a habit I'd like to kick — with both feet.

Withdrawal symptoms

62 When he has withdrawal symptoms it still takes hours for him to leave.

Lonely

63 Talk about lonely. He robbed a bank and even the FBI didn't want him.

Hermit

64 He once resolved never to go where he wasn't wanted, but a few weeks of being a hermit cured him of that.

Ideal host

65 He's the ideal host. He's so ungracious nobody is ever tempted to go to his boring parties.

Invited

66 The only place he's ever invited is outside.

Eye-opener

67 It's an eye-opener to hear him and find what an eyecloser he is.

Trite and true

68 He is found to be trite and true.
    He's not tried and true, but he's trite it's true.

Short visit

69 When she comes for a short visit it's here today and gone tomorrow.

Birthday party

70 They made certain everybody had a good time at his birthday party. They didn't invite him.

Suppose that your most-hated monologist has stopped talking for an instant so that you can interject:

Open and shut

71 It's an open and shut case that your mouth is an open and never shut case.

Unwanted

72 The only time you receive a welcome at anyone's front door is when you're leaving.

Diminishing returns

73 You're such a bore you make me believe in the law of diminishing returns.

Trying to hear

74 What you're trying to say I find trying to hear.

Endurance record

75 Your mouth has just set the world's endurance record.

Muffler shop

76 Why don't you take your mouth into a muffler shop?

History repeats

77 I don't know whether history repeats itself, but you certainly do.

Mouth freshener

78 You need a mouth freshener. Everything that comes out of it now is stale.

Pleasure of company

79 I would like the pleasure of your company, but it only gives me displeasure.

Outspoken

80 You've never been outspoken. No one has ever been able to.

Can't remember

81 I can't remember the last time you opened your mouth. All I know is, you haven't closed it since.

Don't stop fast

82 At that speed you'd better not stop your mouth too fast or your teeth will fly through your cranium.

BRAIN

Brain transplant

83 You need a brain transplant.

Tax brain

84 If you ever tax your brain, don't charge more than a penny.

Brain cavity

85 His dentist found he had one cavity — where his brain should be.

Brain children

86 He has many brain children. But none ever reach maturity.

Brain wave

87 The only brain wave you've ever had is when it waved goodbye.

Empty feeling

88 Don't you have a terribly empty feeling — in your skull?

CANDY

Medicine

89 Sometimes medicine tastes like candy. He's a candy that tastes like medicine.

CHARM

All charm

90 You're all charm. That's all. You've got nothing except charm.

CONGRATULATIONS

Couldn't happen

91 Congratulations! It couldn't happen to a better man. But I wish it had.

CRABBINESS

Murmur maid

92 My wife's a murmur maid.

Crabbing

93 Some people enjoy lobstering. He prefers crabbing.

DEATH WISH

Hit road

94 Why don't you hit the road — fall out of a moving car?

Baser instincts

95 You have nothing to fear from my baser instincts. It's my finer ones that tell me to kill you.

Nine lives

96 I wish he did have nine lives so I'd have the pleasure of taking every one of them.

Your life

97 It's your life. But I wish you'd let us have it.

Grant's tomb

98 They've got the wrong man in Grant's Tomb. It should be you.

Hanging

99 The next time you don't know what to do with yourself, I'd recommend hanging.

Blood

100 You should donate your blood for the good of humanity. Just let it pour out anyplace.

Funeral plot

101 I'll give you a free funeral plot — if you'll promise to move right in.

Vulture

102 I don't consider you a vulture. I consider you something a vulture would eat.

Live for moment

103 I think you should live for the moment. But after that I doubt I'll think so.

Last mile

104 You're the type of person I'd be glad to walk the last mile with — if the warden would let me.

Man alive

105 Man alive! — but I wish you weren't.

Respect for dead

106 I believe in respect for the dead. In fact, I could only respect
you if you were dead.

Really living

107 Man, you're really living! More's the pity.

Graveside

108 You do have a pleasant side, but I'd rather see your graveside.

Iron in system

109 People need iron in their system. But lead would be better in
yours.

DISHONESTY

Petty larceny

110 Any larceny you commit, no matter how big, is petty.

Committed person

111 He's a committed person — once for theft and once for grand
larceny.

Police car

112 There's a police car. Just don't act natural.

Grand larceny

113 To someone you've caught in a dishonest act: You think any
larceny is grand.

Courage

114 I respect you because I've never had the courage it takes to be
a liar, a thief and a cheat.

Immorality

115 The only evidence of your humanity is your extreme immorality.

Wicked

116 Nobody has the right to call you wicked. You're too bad for that.

Kingly manner

117 You behave in a kingly manner, by robbing, stealing and plun-
dering.

Tapeworm

118 If there's an ounce of decency in you, you've got a tapeworm.

DIZZINESS

Bats in belfry

119 What is making you dizzy is not butterflies in the belly but bats in the belfry.

DOCTORS

Suppose that you've just received the doctor's bill:

Maternity bill

120 I don't know whether the stork brings babies, but I do know the maternity bill comes from a rookery.

Symptoms

121 Symptoms: Face flushed. Nervous jitters. Hot under the collar. Diagnosis: You've just seen your doctor, or got his bill.

Trouble

122 When you see a doctor you're in trouble.

Health racket

123 With so many crooks in the health racket, it just isn't healthy to get sick.

DRINKING

Handshakers

124 He's one of those hearty handshakers — and, boy, you should hear his glass rattle!

Alcoholics Anonymous

125 If you want to join Alcoholics Anonymous, I'll oblige by pretending I don't know you.

Lit up

126 He brightens his environment wherever he goes. He's always lit up.

Nip in air

127 There's a nip in the air, so either stop drinking or shut your mouth.

Can't stand you

128 I can't stand you when you've been drinking. I need a hoist.

Chinese water torture

129   You think the Chinese water torture consisted of having to drink nothing but water.

Hates liquor

130   He must hate liquor because he kills all of it he can find.

Anti-Pollution League

131   The Anti-Pollution League has been after him ever since he discovered alcohol.

Her Highness

132   I call her Her Highness because she's always drunk.

Loaded breath

133   When he's been drinking he doesn't say much, but his breath says loads.

Settled in joints

134   I call him Rheumatism because he's settled in the joints.

Give up drinking

135   I'm going to get you to give up drinking. I'll save your life if it kills you.

Alcoholism

136   Joe: "You're an alcoholic." Bill: "I'll drink to that."

Punitive measure

137   You're such a drinker that you consider a mere quart of whiskey a punitive measure.

138   **EPITHETS**

Suppose that you prefer something even more succinct than one-liner insults. Then try some of these:

Dearthgirth	Droughtmouth
Blindmind	Muchmouth
Faminehead	Deaddome
Leadhead	Blankbrain
Shoddybody	Densedome
Perpetual emotion	Monsoon mouth
Barrenbrain	Thunderhead

EVIL

I.Q.

139 I'm glad you have a low I.Q. Think of how much more evil you could be if you were smart.

Acquitting self

140 You're acquitting yourself in such a way that no jury ever would.

Rotten to core

141 You're rotten to the core. And the core is indescribably worse.

Know what you're doing

142 The only time you know what you're doing is when you're doing something evil.

FACE

Facial tissue

143 May I take some of your facial tissue — about ten fingernails' worth?

Ugly personality

144 Your face looks good on you. You've got an ugly personality to go with it.

Only a mother

145 He's got a face only a mother could love — and she hates it.

Chutzpah

146 You certainly have chutzpah.
Who else could wear that face and get away with it?

Broken mirrors

147 Whether your face breaks mirrors I haven't a clue,
But I am certain it has made you break quite a few.

FAILURES

Failing years

148 He's been in his failing years ever since he started school.

First in field

149 You're the first in your field — starting from the bottom.

Err-do-well

150 He's a ne'er-do-well and an err-do-well.

Bottoms up

151   His motto is bottoms up. That's the only way a bum can make it to the top.

Sure things

152   He bets on only sure things. Any horse he bets on is sure to lose.

Given others a start

153   You've never gotten anyplace, but you've sure given other people a start.

Piano lessons

154   He took piano lessons but did so poorly the teacher made him give them back.

Good loser

155   He's a good loser. In fact, that's all he does.

Plot against you

156   The only reason you're not a success is that there's a plot against you. All the forces of reason are arrayed against you.

Fails in light

157   He never strikes out blindly. He fails in the light.

Strike out

158   He went out on his own. He didn't need any help to strike out.

Suppose that you're asked about a fellow's chances of success. Reply:

Comeback

159   Talk about failures — if he were to make a comeback, he'd be at the bottom.

Wildest dreams

160   The only thing standing between him and his wildest dreams of success is the reality of his inferiority.

Break in leg

161   Talk about a loser! The only time he got a break, it was in the leg.

Filthy rich

162   He's well on his way to becoming filthy rich. Already he's filthy.

Blaze of failure

163 He's going down in a blaze of failure.

FAMILY

Good family

164 He came from a good family (I say "came" because they would-n't keep him).

Orphan

165 If you were orphaned when you were a child, I feel sorry for you — but not for your parents.

Intelligent children

166 You must have intelligent children. How else could they have survived such a dumb parent?

Illegitimate children

167 If you don't want to give people a bad name you'll have your kids illegitimately.

Kidnapped kid

168 He was kidnapped as a child but returned because his parents couldn't pay enough.

Big cluck

169 Is it true your mother is a chicken because she gave the world a big cluck?

Respect parents

170 He doesn't respect his parents. But who *could* respect his par-ents after what they did to the world?

FATNESS

Found wanting

171 She's been weighed and found wanting — too much ice cream, candy and cake.

Feed stomach

172 I don't know why I feed my stomach. It doesn't do anything for me.

Consumption

173 She has the disease of consumption.

A lot in clothes
174 She puts a lot into clothes — about 200 pounds.

Billows
175 With his stomach he billows into sight.

Ballooning
176 The way she's ballooning, at 10,000 feet she'll explode.

Suppose that someone comments adversely about your physical appearance. You counterattack with one or more of the following:

Too fat
177 I wouldn't say you're too fat. I'll let your doctor do that.

Tidal wave
178 I'd tell you to go jump in the ocean, but I don't want to start a tidal wave.

Mississippi
179 I hear there was a bad flood along the Mississippi recently. Did you really go in bathing?

Good Texan
180 You'd sure make a good Texan with that big spread.

Candy
181 Candy certainly gives you a bad hangover — your belt.

Fleshpots
182 If you want to make the acquaintance of one of the world's great fleshpots, just pat your stomach.

Carry weight well
183 You carry your weight surprisingly well. From the looks of you, I've been expecting you to collapse.

Wheel
184 When are you going to get a wheel to put under your stomach?

Blubbering
185 Stop blubbering, you whale! Melt some of it.

Glutton for punishment
186 You're a glutton for punishment. Anyone as fat as you should be punished.

Figure 37

You're a glutton for punishment. Anyone as piggish as you should be punished.

Losing head
187 Don't lose your head — I don't see any point in your losing twenty pounds of ugly fat.

FEMALES

Protective instinct
188 Women bring out the protective instinct in me. I feel I must protect myself from them.

High opinion
189 I have an unjustifiably high opinion of women. I consider them idiots.

Born a woman
190 I find women are good for cheering me up. Whenever I feel depressed, I just remember that I might have been born a woman.

Insulting someone
191 I feel like insulting someone. Do you mind if I call you a woman?

Spokesman for women
192 Anyone who becomes a spokesman for women has to be loud and longwinded.

Used to be
193 It's true I'm not the man I used to be. But you were never the woman you used to be.

Rib
194 You're one female who looked better as a rib.
Why don't you crawl back into the ribcage where you belong?

FIGURE

Youthful figure
195 You have a youthful figure — round and dumpy like a baby's.

Own image
196 Many people want to shape the world in their own image. She doesn't — they're already in the same bad shape.

FILTH

Hippie

197 If you ask a hippie to take a bath, he's likely to say, "Okay, but no soap."

Not Sanforized

198 He claims he doesn't take a bath because he isn't Sanforized and doesn't want to shrink.

Cultured man

199 He's a cultured man — lots of germs growing on him.

Pig sty

200 Someone said you live in an apartment. I said, "In a pig sty, he does."

FOOD

Castoffs

201 What are these steaks — castoffs from dog food?

One more thing

202 This dish of yours needed just one more thing in order to be superb — a good cook!

Swine

203 My wife must think I'm a swine. She feeds me nothing but garbage.

Tea leaves

204 I can read these tea leaves. They tell me you're a lousy tea maker.

FORGETFULNESS

Amnesia

205 He's got amnesia. He'll deny it, but then it's so bad he's forgotten he has it.

FRIENDS

Feathered friends

206 He has some fine feathered friends — with some tar mixed in.

Loyal to friends

207 He's loyal to his friends. His friends are vices.

GARBAGE

Strain yourself

208 Don't strain yourself. Garbage usually doesn't.

GENOCIDE

Not murder

209 If you were to kill everybody who hates you, it wouldn't be murder. It would be genocide.

GOLD DIGGERS

Drop of pin

210 She'll fall for any man at the drop of a pin — if it's got enough diamonds in it.

After all

211 After all, when it comes to men, she's after all.

GOSSIP

Too early to tell

212 With her it's never too early to tell — or too bad.

Rundown feeling

213 Gossip? Everyone she talks to leaves with a rundown feeling.

Day of silence

214 My wife decided there would be no more gossip in her conversation. But one day of silence cured her of that.

Board and rumors

215 She serves board and rumors.

Spreads dirt

216 She not only digs up the past — she then spreads the dirt around.

Reckless driver

217 Her tongue is a reckless driver. It's always running people down.

Alarmist

218 She's an alarmist system.

Rundown

219 My wife has given me the rundown on everyone she knows, and boy, can she ever run them down!

HAIR

Hair-raising experience

220   He has so many wide open spaces on his head, he's praying for a hair-raising experience.

HARD UP

Throw a party

221   I'd like to throw her a party. But he won't let me.

Wedding present

222   She's not particular about what wedding present she receives. Any man will do.

Best behavior

223   When he first takes a girl out he usually belches, swears, picks his nose and spits on the floor. But that's only because, on the first date, he wants to be on his best behavior.

Worship from afar

224   A lot of women worship him from afar. It's only when they get close that they hate him.

Lipstick

225   Hard up for men, she makes her lipstick out of flypaper glue — to no avail.

Take or leave alone

226   He can either take girls or leave them alone, because taking them is the only way he can get them.

Fan mail

227   His girls send him lots of fan mail — all of it giving him the breeze.

Best friend

228   Even his best friend cheats and lies to him. But that's the best friend he can get.

Fragile package

229   She's a fragile package but likes being manhandled.

Soul-searching

230   You should do some soul-searching. Maybe you'll find one.

Suppose that you're engaged in a little boyish (or girlish) back-biting with a friend. A subject that is certain to be discussed soon-

er or later is the mutual acquaintance who has a hard time with the opposite sex:

Pity

231 I'd marry her out of pity if I didn't have more pity on myself.

One mistake

232 Everybody is entitled to at least one mistake. Otherwise no one will ever marry him.

Stone her

233 The only way he can ever get a date with a girl is to stone her — about 50 carats' worth.

Popular with men

234 She's popular with the men — every last one of him.

Run down

235 Every time he looks for a date he manages to run one down. That's the only way she'll get in the car with him.

Sex drive

236 The overwhelming power of the sex drive is demonstrated by the fact that someone was willing to father her kids.

Blind

237 If a man said he loved her, she'd either have to be blind to believe it or he'd have to be blind to mean it.

Bachelor

238 He may not be the world's most eligible bachelor, but he's the most rejected.

Eyes closed

239 All of his girls kiss with their eyes closed. Considering his face, that's the only way they could.

Squeal

240 The girls he dates never squeal on him. But with their looks you expect it at any moment.

Desperate

241 Some girls want to marry him desperately. They have to be desperate to want to.

HATE
Worst of me
242 You'll never get the best of me — only the worst, my hate.

Remind of mistakes
243 I think nature obviously hates you because you remind it of its mistakes.

So much to hate
244 I love you because you give me so much to hate.

Express opinion
245 I'm very careful how I express my opinion of you because I want to put as much vituperation as possible in it.

Special place
246 You have a special place in my heart. I don't hate anyone else as much as I do you.

HEADS
Soft head
247 With your head you've got it soft.

Solid head
248 You've got a solid head. You don't seem to be afraid of anything except woodpeckers.

Coffee head
249 Your head is like coffee — vacuum packed.

Childhood trauma
250 Don't hold his behavior against him. It was caused by childhood trauma, when he fell on his head and his parents spanked him for breaking the cement.

HEALTH NUTS
Health lecturers
251 Health lecturers have something wrong with their digestive tracts — the ones they write.

HEART
Magnetometer
252 The only way to detect whether you have a heart is with a magnetometer.

HELL
Blaze a way

253 In the next life you'll blaze a way for us to enjoy.

Welcome

254 You welcome everybody the way death will welcome you —
with a blast of hot air.

HENPECKED
Own voice

255 He's so henpecked he hasn't heard his own voice in five years.

Speak up

256 He was so henpecked that when he finally did speak up he was
frightened not only by his courage but by the sound of his voice.

Practical wife

257 She's a practical wife with her feet planted firmly on her husband.

Doghouse

258 He's master in his own house — the doghouse.

HOMELINESS
Say boo

259 If I were really as ugly as you
Instead of saying hello I'd say boo.

Wig

260 That wig you're wearing looks good. It's what is attached to the
bottom that makes it ugly.

Fix face

261 When joining a beauty contest she fixes her face
But the only way she could win is to fix the race.

Stops looking

262 When a bachelor sees her he stops looking. No women look good
to him after that.

Not without pity

263 I'm not a person without pity. I do feel sorry for you because
you're so homely, but I feel even sorrier for the rest of us because
you are.

Ugh

264   You're ugh stuff.

Rare beauty

265   You're a woman of rare beauty. We've never seen it.

Mirror

266   When women look in the mirror and see a homely face they go to the beauty parlor. In your case I'd suggest you and mirrors go separate ways.

Case of ugliness

267   Yours is a prima facie case of ugliness. But your body is ugly, too.

Really ugly

268   I know you should judge a man by what he really is instead of only by appearances. But you're really ugly.

Ugly kit

269   They say she's really a beautiful girl. If so, I'd like to know where she bought her ugly kit.

Things

270   Things are never what they seem. Isn't it nice to know you're not ugly?

Suppose that you're trading personal insults with a good friend, or even a poor one. Use some of these to test his (or her) friendship:

Hated looks

271   I've hated your looks from the start they gave me.

Lose his head

272   Many a man has been made to lose his head over a girl by moonlight. In your case it would take moonshine.

Ugly license

273   Don't you need a license to be that ugly?

Collision

274   When you meet the eye it's with a collision.

Artificial ugliness

275   I may look ugly, but at least my ugliness is natural. Yours is artificial.

Moonlight

276 Moonlight becomes you — total darkness even more.

Ugly body

277 I don't know which would be worse, to live with your ugly body or in it.

Suppose that someone has tried to elicit a compliment by coyly belittling his (or her) own looks. You tug at the bait:

Painful

278 People can't complain about your looks. They know it's painful enough for you, just having them.

Kind of cute

279 You are kind of cute. But it's an ugly kind.

Make you rich

280 Your looks could make you rich. Just stand on a corner with your hat in your hand.

Picture

281 I took a photo of you once, but it didn't turn out. You could be seen too clearly.

Your sake

282 I hope for your sake you're not as ugly as you look.

Face transplant

283 You're so ugly you should get a face transplant.

HUMOR

Good jokes

284 He tells good jokes — they've proven their popularity for thousands of years.

Blush

285 Every time you tell me a joke I blush, but not for me.

No wit

286 You unwittingly told a joke. There was no wit in it.

Dry humor

287 He has a dry humor. In fact, it's as boring as can be.

Last laugh

288 He managed to get the last laugh — a long time ago.

Composer

289   I compose jokes. When you tell them, you decompose them.

Toss out

290   You should toss out more of your funny remarks. That's all they're good for.

Uproariously funny

291   I think that's uproariously funny! Not your joke — the fact that you thought it was funny.

ILLITERACY

Signature

292   "Where did he sign his signature?"
        "*X* marks the spot."

IMMORALITY

Christian friends

293   I'm sure you have only good Christians for friends. Anyone who could like you must be able to love anything.

Morals

294   Your life history has no morals to the story.

Alexander the Great

295   He's like Alexander the Great. He has made many conquests and will die of an unspeakable disease.

Lady of pleasure

296   She's a lady of pleasure who looks as though she's been over-joyed.

All men love

297   All men love that actress. Well, maybe a few haven't had a chance yet.

Great store

298   She sets great store by her virtue. That's why she charges so much for it.

Basically good

299   Basically you're a good person. As base as one can get.

Few have known

300 She's shared a love with him that few have ever known — maybe only a hundred or so.

Degenerative disease

301 He must have a degenerative disease. It's certainly made him degenerate.

IMPRISONMENT

Serving time

302 This world would be so sublime
If instead of guff you were serving time.

INFERIORITY

Has nothing

303 You can't say he has nothing. After all, he does have inferiority.

Low opinion

304 You must have a low opinion of people if you think they're your equals.

Worthlessness

305 When I'm near you I get a feeling of worthlessness — but then I realize you were born that way.

Think about you

306 Of course I don't think about you. It's beneath me to think about things beneath me.

INSANITY

All here

307 I wish you were all here. I don't like to think there's more.

Right mind

308 If you're in your right mind, I pray you'll go insane.

Nuts

309 Are you being helped? Or are you going to go on being nuts?

Off days

310 He has his really off days, but he's always a little off.

INSULTS

Love my fellow man

311 The only time I love my fellow man is when I've just dreamed up a first-class insult.

Pan-handler

312 I'm a pan-handler. I know how to handle insults.

Mouth

313 Here's a question your mouth always poses:
Does it bite the hardest when it opens or when it closes?

JABS

Help

314 May I help you? No, come to think of it, nothing could help you.

Dirt in eye

315 If I told you I have a piece of dirt in my eye, would you move?

What in world

316 What in the world were you doing — before you crawled out?

Find himself

317 He's still trying to find himself. If he ever succeeds, the shock will be so great he'll have to get amnesia to survive.

Unsure of identity

318 He's disturbed because he's unsure of his identity. Think of what he'd be if he knew what he really is.

Foundry

319 Why don't you start a foundry? You've got enough brass.

Accept you

320 Do you want me to accept you as you are or do you want me to like you?

Knowing you

321 I wouldn't trade knowing you for anything. I'd have to make sure, first, that what I was getting wasn't just as terrible.

Darndest thing

322 I just heard the darndest thing — and you're still talking.

Swine

323 If you were a swine you'd be what you are now.

Shooting for

324   I'm something worth shooting for. You're something worth shooting at.

Bad name

325   Your parents gave you a bad name, but not nearly as bad as the one you're giving them.

Everywhere-nowhere

326   I've been everywhere, so I can tell you, man, you're from nowhere!

Someone else

327   You wouldn't be nearly as bad as you are if you were someone else.

Pleasant day

328   "I want to thank you for giving me such a pleasant day."
"But I haven't been with you."
"That's what I mean."

Troubles

329   I don't know why I tell you my troubles. You've got a big problem: yourself.

Comedownance

330   You'll eventually get your comedownance.

Only life

331   Remember, it may not be much, but it's the only life you've got. Thank heavens!

Death and taxes

332   I take you for granted — like death and taxes.

Merry-go-round

333   His mother forgot to take him off the merry-go-round when he was a kid and he's been going round and round ever since.

Monotony

334   I'd like to break the monotony. Where's your weakest point?

Perfume

335   You're like an expensive perfume — a little bit of you goes a long way.

Threat to ego
336   I don't want to associate with you because you're a threat to my ego — I might be seen with you.

Love thee
337   The question is not "How do I love thee," but rather, "How could I love thee?"

Life's work
338   He's one of the few men who are happy in their life's work. His is making people miserable.

Right from wrong
339   You certainly know right from wrong. Otherwise, you couldn't be so consistently wrong.

Good eyesight
340   You've got good eyesight — you see enemies everywhere.

Mistaken identity
341   Yours is a case of mistaken identity. It was a great mistake for nature to make you what you are.

Fix your wagon
342   I wish I were a carpenter so I could fix your wagon.

Standout
343   He's a standout in any crowd. They make him stand out.

Identity crisis
344   She has an identity crisis. No one will recognize her.

Solipsists
345   Solipsists say that what we see and feel and hear may not really be there. You're enough to make me hope they're right.

Pollution
346   Like most other Americans, I'm concerned about the pollution of my environment. Please leave it.

Daylight
347   I'd like to whale the daylight into you.

Flattering
348   It's flattering to have you hate me. It makes me seem more important than I really am.

Answer to prayer

349 You're the answer to my prayer — I prayed to find out if things could get worse.

Perfect trip

350 I thought about you while I was on vacation, so it wasn't a perfect trip.

Obnoxious

351 At least you're not obnoxious like so many other people — you're obnoxious in a different and worse way.

No threat

352 Men and women like you for good reason — you're no threat to either of them.

New York

353 She crossed New York by going to live in it.

JOB

Tragic ending

354 I had a friend who came to a tragic ending. He got a job here.

Kind employer

355 He's so kind he can't even discharge an employee — he retires them without pay.

Fit as fiddler

356 He's fit as a fiddler, but not as a worker.

Out of a job

357 He never works himself out of a job. Since he never works, he can't hold one.

Travel on job

358 I got tired of the same old work on my job, so I asked my boss to let me travel. He sent me packing.

Can't figure out

359 I can't figure out what you're doing here today. I know why you're here, but not what you're doing.

KILLING

Well wishers

360 You have lots of well wishers. They'd all like to throw you down one.

Fool's paradise

361   You're one man who's not living in a fool's paradise — but many people would like to send you there.

LATENESS

Impromptu

362   Everything he does is impromptu. He's never prompt.

LAWYER

Lawyer

363   A lawyer is a man who advises his clients on how not to lose all they own to anyone but him.

LAZINESS

Through and through

364   He's a worker through and through — a long time ago.

Two-cycle engine

365   When it comes to washing walls he's like a two-cycle engine — two strokes and he's exhausted.

Busybody

366   For such a busybody she's sure lazy.

Incompetence

367   He does everything effortlessly. That's why it's done so poorly.

Getting work done

368   I'm not having any trouble getting my work done. It's your work I'm having trouble with.

Afraid to sleep

369   He's been afraid to sleep ever since he had a nightmare about working.

Special event

370   He's going to a special event. He's going to work, and for him that's a special event.

Talented man

371   He's a talented man who can do a little of everything. In fact, he's so talented at being lazy that he gets away with doing almost nothing of everything.

Work hard

372 I work hard. It's always hard to make me work.

Never do another thing

373 One time a feeling of languor came over him and he felt as though he'd like to never do another thing. That was when he was a baby, and the feeling has been with him ever since.

Afraid of death

374 He was always afraid of death until he heard someone call it "going to your rest."

Let his hair grow

375 He's so lazy it wears him out just to let his hair grow.

Idleness worshipper

376 I'm not an idol worshipper, but I am an idleness worshipper.

Suppose that you're a foreman — a very tolerant, good-natured, compassionate, lovable foreman who hardly ever loses his temper — but once in a while you just can't control yourself. Maybe one of these will come in handy:

Catch in act

377 I'll never catch you in the act — any act!

Performed well

378 The only thing you've ever performed well is acting as though you're working.

Declining reclining

379 I'll never find you declining reclining.

Goofing

380 When you're not goofing off, you're goofing.

The least

381 The least you can do is what you do.

Done wrong

382 You may not do much work, but what you do is always done wrong.

Won't do

383 You won't do — anything.

Not responsible

384 Whenever there's a mistake and someone says you're responsible, I say you're not. You're not responsible about anything.

Long time

385 It takes you a long time to get around to doing something, but when you do you do it wrong.

Lazy pills

386 How many lazy pills did you take today?

Work-prone

387 You're a work-prone person. When it comes to work, you're always lying down.

Idly by

388 You're always standing idly by.

Works hard

389 You work hard at whatever you do. It's hard for you to do anything.

Smile in sleep

390 You must smile in your sleep, you enjoy it so.

LIES

Dishonest

391 He's so dishonest you can't even be sure that what he's telling you is a lie.

Hotbed of lies

392 You've lived in such a hotbed of lies and cheating, that's what you'll have in the next life.

Slander

393 Slander is an untrue detraction of you;
Thus it is useless, since the truth would do.

Little something extra

394 He has gotten rich by giving his clients a little something extra — lies.

Doubt veracity

395 I must say I don't doubt your veracity — but, then, I'm as big a liar as you are.

Lie for the day
396 I'm willing to concede you're brilliant. I haven't yet told my lie for the day.

Only time
397 The only time he tells the truth is when it's an insult.

LIPSTICK
Loudmouth
398 That lipstick gives you a loudmouth.

LOGIC
Vacate premises
399 Let's not say your logic is wrong. Let's just suggest you vacate your premises immediately.

LOOKS
Likeness
400 I don't like your likeness.

Knockout looks
401 He has knockout looks. Anyone seeing them wants to knock him out.

Defend your looks
402 Even Edward Bennett Williams couldn't defend your looks.

Handsome as anything
403 You're as handsome as anything — and I do mean any old thing.

Plain to see
404 It's plain to see you're plain to see.

Ran into door
405 Now I suppose you're going to tell me you ran into a door? I know you don't have a black eye, but that face couldn't have happened naturally.

Plain tired
406 I'm just plain tired. You're just plain.

Hairshirts
407 I wish I had your looks to help me do penance. I've sinned and they don't sell hairshirts anymore.

Grows on you
408   She has the kind of face that grows on you — but I wish it hadn't on her.

Startled me
409   You startled me. For a minute I thought you were wearing a mask.

Graven image
410   Yours is a graven image. It looks dead.

Weapon
411   She has a weapon against molesters — her face.

MATE

To the victor
412   To the victor goes the spoiled.

In trouble
413   She stays with her husbands when they're in trouble — because they're in trouble when she stays with them.

Smart-stupid
414   He thinks girls like him because he's smart, when it's just that they're stupid.

Anxious to see wife
415   Everybody's anxious to see my beautiful, intelligent, young wife. I am too.

Source of hope
416   She's a source of hope for single people. If she could get a spouse, anybody can.

Ancient ruins
417   I don't like being a tourist and seeing ancient ruins — especially when mine insists on coming with me.

New fur coat
418   When his wife said she wanted a new fur coat, he bought her a hair grower.

Bunch of drunks
419   She married a bunch of drunks. They had to be drunk to marry her.

Mother-in-law trouble

420 I have mother-in-law trouble. She's a wonderful woman, but she gave birth to my wife.

Sacrifice young maidens

421 Talk about voodoo! Even here in America they have religious ceremonies in which they sacrifice young maidens to satisfy the demons. Your wedding was one of them.

Best years of life

422 When my wife told me she'd given me the best years of her life, I replied that I'd given her the best years of her life and the worst of mine.

Suppose that you're having a night out with the boys, and naturally the conversation gets around to the wives. Outclass the other fellows with some of these:

Two-faced

423 My wife's so two-faced I feel like a bigamist.

Troubleshooter

424 I told my wife I wanted to become a troubleshooter, but decided she wasn't worth it.

Supply and demand

425 Our budget is a case of supply and demand. I supply and she demands.

Stuck by my side

426 My wife has always stuck by my side whenever things go wrong. After all, she makes them that way.

Great desirability

427 My wife has great desirability. She desires more than anyone I know.

Together in death

428 My wife and I have adjoining burial plots so we can be together in death. It's this being together in life that I can't stand.

Not fortunate

429 My wife never talks to me. No, I'm not fortunate — she screams.

Tender

430 The only time my wife was tender was when she got sunburned.

Tetanus shot

431   I gave my wife a tetanus shot but she still doesn't have lockjaw.

Nanny

432   My wife gets my nanny cause I'm her goat.

Compromiser

433   My wife is a great compromiser. If we can afford a Chevrolet and she wants a Cadillac, she'll settle for a Chrysler.

Commanding presence

434   My wife has a commanding presence.

Wifetime of misery

435   I've had a wifetime of misery.

Groping for love

436   I was groping blindly in the dark for love until I met my wife. Shows what you can come up with when you can't see.

Suppose that you're still out for an evening with the boys — or with the boys and your wives. The conversation is bound to include some juicy tidbits of gossip about somebody who isn't there, such as the following:

Good reason to marry

437   There's a good reason why he should want to marry such a homely woman. He'd never be sorry to lose her.

Good qualities

438   She's capable, intelligent, and everything else a man could ever need — but nothing he'd want.

Grow old with

439   He's a man for a woman to grow old with — in a hurry.

Content to be alone

440   She thinks of him when she's lonely. Then she's content to be alone.

Act of mercy

441   He married her as an act of mercy — to other men.

Best years of life

442   She gave him the best years of her life. So you can understand why he doesn't want to stick around for the worst.

Like a god

443 His wife treats him like a god — she gives him ten percent of all he earns.

Running ragged

444 His wife is running him ragged — they go out so often he can't afford anything better.

Scrapbook

445 He has a scrapbook to record his marriage — every one of them.

In mourning

446 She's in mourning for her husband. He's still alive.

MIND

Sixth sense

447 You'd have to have a sixth sense not only to read his mind, but to even detect if he has one.

One-track mind

448 He's got such a one-track mind that his encephalograph shows a permanent wave.

Piece of mind

449 For two cents I'd give you a piece of my mind — and all of yours.

Mind of my own

450 She thinks I need a mind of my own, so she keeps giving me some of hers.

Filthy mind

451 His mind is filthy — and yet it's sterile.

Lost mind

452 You haven't lost your mind — alas.

Only thing

453 The only thing that's ever crossed your mind is itself.

Concentrates mind

454 When he concentrates his mind there's still no sign of it.

MISTAKES

Perfect record

455 You've got a perfect record — 100 percent errors.

Holier than I

456   You're not holier than I, but your arguments have a lot more holes than mine.

Blunders

457   I can't say you never do anything right. After all, you commit your blunders with superb efficiency.

Perfect mistakes

458   Everything you do isn't incompetent. You do make mistakes with perfection.

Making ends meet

459   She has no trouble making ends meet. Her foot is always in her mouth.

Profit by mistakes

460   Here's an easy way for you to get rich: Learn to profit by your mistakes.

MOUTH

Mouth

461   You could have a beautiful mouth — all you'd have to do is close it.

Poormouthing

462   You're always poormouthing! Everything coming out of your mouth is poor.

NAG

Married to a nag

463   "He's married to a nag."
      "Is she always telling him what's wrong with him?"
      "Why, no, how could she? She's a horse."

Nagging doubts

464   My wife doesn't have any nagging doubts. She never hesitates; she just nags and nags.

NIGHTMARES

Bad trip

465   You look like something out of a bad trip.

OLD FASHIONED
Keeping in step
466 He's keeping in step with the past times.
Living fossil
467 You're a living fossil.

OLDNESS
Honest face
468 You have an honest face. It admits it's old.
Wisdom of ages
469 I have the wisdom of the ages; you, of the aged.
Time on hands
470 It's better to have time on your hands than on your face.
Senile
471 At least you act your age — senile.
Not the half of it
472 She has the nerve to say she's 39. But that's not the half of it.
Home for the aged
473 Let's face it. Your body is a home for the aged.
Die of old age
474 I think I'm going to die of old age — my wife's.
Amazing
475 You say you're forty? That's amazing! You still look as though you're only fifty.

OPINIONATED
Without a doubt
476 You are, without a doubt . . .
Unprejudiced
477 He's unprejudiced — by the facts.
Sticks by convictions
478 You're a man who sticks by his convictions. You'll remain a fool no matter how much you get ridiculed for it.

Express opinions

479   At least he can express his opinions with certainty. He knows they're wrong.

Check your religion

480   Check your religion — then don't redeem it.

Another opinion

481   Why don't you get another opinion — your own?

Doubly cursed

482   You're doubly cursed with your beliefs. They're not only wrong, they're unpopularly wrong.

PAIN

Novocain

483   A dope you are and will remain.
Completely unlike Novocain.
You add to, not diminish, pain.

PENNYPINCHING

Dirties hands

484   He dirties his hands over and over again with money — the same money.

Handful of deadbeats

485   You're one of that handful of deadbeats about whom it can be said, "Never have so few owed so much to so many."

Coin in fountain

486   If you threw a coin in the fountain you'd wish it had been a slug.

Vest pocket

487   He wears a vest pocket so he can keep his money close to his heart.

Charges everything

488   He charged his car battery the other day. In fact, he charges everything he buys.

Takes for granted

489   He takes for granted that taking's for granted.

Tight?

490   Tight? The only reason he wants to live to be a hundred is to beat the pension system.

Pretty penny

491 He's spent a pretty penny on girls. But that's about all he's spent.

Deadbeats

492 His money doesn't stretch very far, but his checks do.

Church

493 He contributes a great deal to his church. He doesn't go.

Any penny is pretty

494 He resents paying a pretty penny for anything. Any penny is pretty to him.

Take it easy

495 He knows how to take it easy. Giving is what he finds hard.

Forgetting

496 He's always forgetting but never for giving.

Weak dollars

497 My dollars are weak from inflation, yours from getting no exercise.

PERSONALITY

Multiple personalities

498 You've got multiple personalities — all repulsive.

Arrest development

499 Considering what you're becoming, I'm going to call a cop and arrest your development.

PRETENSE

Greatest show

500 Your pretense is the greatest show on earth.

False personality

501 Your personality is as false as your teeth.

Artificial people

502 He's not one of these artificial people. No, sir! People hate him for himself.

Hate me for myself

503 I don't believe in being artificial. I want people to hate me for myself.

REPULSIVENESS

Genuine person

504   You're a genuine person. Your repulsiveness is real.

Doesn't agree

505   Food doesn't agree with you? What or who does?

Accomplishes the impossible

506   He accomplishes the impossible — he keeps getting more repulsive.

Looking at you

507   One way of looking at you is that you're evil. In fact, any way of looking at you...

REPUTATION

Live down

508   You'll never be able to live down to your reputation.

RETORTS

Suppose that while you're entertaining, someone keeps interjecting unwanted comments or otherwise irritating you. You squelch him or her as follows:

Intelligent conversation

509   Let's have an intelligent conversation. I'll talk and you listen.

Two-cents' worth

510   You're always putting in your two-cents' worth — at inflated rates, of course.

Don't consider source

511   When you insult me, I don't consider the source. It isn't worth considering.

Worth a darn

512   Someone said you aren't worth a darn. I say you are — and some real profanity, to boot!

Won't admit

513   Some places may admit you, but I'll bet your parents don't.

In common

514   I see we have something in common — a great revulsion.

Make me angry

515   You make me so angry I'm inviting you outside. Please leave!

Silence!

516   Silence! Or it will be borne out that you'll be borne out.

Electric chair

517   As the warden said to the man in the electric chair, "More power to you."

Mentally incompetent

518   You've just declared yourself mentally incompetent.

Master of putdown

519   You're certainly a master of the putdown. All you have to do is speak and it's an insult!

Dead bull

520   Don't you think that bull is pretty well dead by now? You've been shooting it long enough.

SELF LOVE

Dislocated arms

521   He won't be in today. He dislocated his arms trying to put them around himself.

Self-image

522   For the sake of your ego I'm glad your self-image isn't the one you see in the mirror.

Eternal triangle

523   It's the eternal triangle — his wife, himself, and his ego.

Conceit

524   You should think a great deal of yourself. Conceited people usually do.

Only person alive

525   Boy, if you were the only person left alive, this would be a world full of love for all mankind!

SELFISHNESS

Self-employed

526   She's self-employed. She works at nothing but thinking of herself.

Greeting

527   Her greeting should be, "Hello, what can you do for me?"

SKIN
Battlements

528   They say the skin is the first defense of the body — and sure
       enough, yours looks like battlements.

Protective skin

529   She has a skin that protects her against germs — and men.

Gaunt

530   He's run the gauntlet. He's as gaunt as one can get.

SMOKING
Chain smoker

531   He's a chain smoker — he's chained to smoking.

Pot smoker

532   She's a pot smoker. Have you ever seen a pot smoking?

Great Smokies

533   Is it true you had a mountain range named after you — the
       Great Smokies?

Smoke signals

534   Heap big smoke-in-the-mouth is sending out smoke signals.
       They say, "I am a fool."

SOURNESS
Sweet as you are

535   Please stay as sweet as you are! Any more sourness would be
       unendurable.

Smile!

536   Smile! The law of gravity only applies to weight.

Surly

537   He's lazy, but he still gets up surly every morning.

Nothing pleasant

538   A lot of delicious, wholesome food has gone into that mouth
       of yours Why doesn't anything pleasant ever come out of it?

Pall-bearer

539 He's a pall-bearer. He casts a pall wherever he goes.

Sweet tooth

540 I know you have a sweet tooth. Now why don't you get a face to go with it?

SPEAKING — SPEECH

Think

541 Think before you speak. Then you won't.

Hole in head

542 Your talk is just a lot of dirt which came from a hole in your head.

Suppose that your wife has forced you to attend a boring lecture. Afterwards she makes the mistake of asking how you liked it, giving you the perfect opportunity to get off one of these:

Took our time

543 He took his time when he talked. Unfortunately he took ours, too!

Soothing

544 He was a soothing speaker, I'll say that. He put me right to sleep.

Get a lot

545 I always get a lot out of his talks — I spend the time thinking about something worthwhile.

Economy of words

546 He practices an economy of words. Unfortunately, the economy is always at full production.

One in a million

547 Every word of his was like a jewel — one in a million.

Great heights

548 His oratory could raise him to great heights if he'd talk into a balloon.

Bunk of America

549 His mouth just opened a new branch of the Bunk of America!

SPECIMEN
Perfect specimen
550 Look at that body and face! Isn't he a perfect specimen? Get a vial and we'll give him to a doctor.

Specimen lab
551 He works all day in a specimen lab. He has tremendous viality.

STATES
Smart enough
552 I'm proud to have come from that state. It shows I was smart enough to leave it.

Nevada
553 Nevada is the gamiest state in the country.

Special rates
554 The railroads have special rates to and from that state — $1 to take you in and a thousand to take you out.

STUPIDITY
Stupid subjects
555 I don't like to talk on stupid subjects — or to them, so don't bother me!

Never argue
556 Those two never argue. One would have to have an intelligent thought before the other could sincerely oppose it.

Gasoline
557 He's so stupid, he bathes in gasoline so he won't get wrinkles.

Moron
558 He does the best he knows how. That's why he has to be considered a moron.

Nature has been good
559 Nature has been good to him. It's made him so stupid he doesn't care that he is.

Dumbbell
560 Everything I say to her seems to ring a bell — a dumbbell.

New experience
561 He couldn't get to sleep because he was thinking. Such a new experience was unsettling.

Suppose that, just for the fun of it, you and a friend decide to exchange insults about your respective intelligence (doing this can be fun!). Divide these up and toss them at each other:

Pretty smart

562 I admire you! You have to be pretty darned smart to get away with being as stupid as you are.

Write a check

563 If you were to write a check against your intelligence, it'd bounce.

Never know

564 You'll never know . . .

Second thought

565 On second thought, you've never had a first one.

Plays the fool

566 He never plays the fool — that's always genuine, never an act.

Know now

567 If you'd known years ago what you know now, you'd have been an idiot then, too.

New way

568 You're an ingenious person. If there's ever a new way to make a fool of yourself, you always find it.

Know something?

569 You know something? Oh, I forgot — you know nothing.

Can't figure out

570 I can't figure you out. I'm not smart enough to think as stupidly as you.

Age of specialization

571 Because it's the age of specialization, did yours have to consist of being an idiot?

Stupefying experience

572 What stupefying experience did you have to make you such a stoop?

Gray matter

573 The only gray matter you've got upstairs is hair.

Forgive me

574 If you'll forgive me for calling you stupid, I'll forgive you for being ignorant.

Village idiot

575 He was the most entertaining man in town — the village idiot.

Hate you

576 I don't hate you for being stupid. There are many worse things than being a fool — and it's those I hate you for.

TALKING

Wish you'd stop

577 Now you're talking! And how I wish you'd stop!

Repulsive talk

578 What makes your talk repulsive is not so much what you say as the way you say it — audibly.

Free silence

579 Why don't you exercise your god-given right of free silence?

Punishment

580 She isn't speaking to me. That's a terrible punishment — to her.

Thought out

581 I wish you were as talked out as you are thought out.

Drag

582 That wind from your mouth is creating a drag — you.

Long story short

583 To make a long story short — is what you never do.

Restaurant sign

584 You should put a restaurant sign on your mouth: "Open 24 hours a day."

No end

585 He loves his own talk, no end.

Skip lip

586 Let's play a little game of skip-the-lip — not trip-the-lip.

Prolong life

587 I'd like to prolong your life — so I'm telling you to shut up.

Sound of voice

588 She becomes so engrossed by the sound of her own voice that she starts listening and stops thinking.

Autonomous nervous system

589 Her tongue has become part of her autonomous nervous system.

Small talk

590 Yours is small talk no matter what the subject is.

Anything to declare

591 Talk about a talker! The customs man asked my wife if she had anything to declare, then couldn't shut her up.

Mouthwash

592 You make me wish they had a mouthwash for words.

Pain

593 You're a pain in the ears!

Hello

594 "The most memorable thing she ever said was 'Hello.' "
"Just 'Hello'?"
"Yes. That's why it was so memorable."

Tasteless

595 Your conversation, like water, is tasteless.

Loose tongue

596 She has a loose tongue. It's disconnected from her brain.

TEARFULNESS
Crying need

597 She has a crying need. Certainly practices it a lot.

Adaptable person

598 He's a very adaptable person — adapts his self-pity to any situation, no matter how pleasant.

Ever since

599 When she was born the doctor spanked her to start her crying, and she hasn't stopped since.

THINKING
Try it

600 Just think! (Try it.)

Premeditated remark

601   That was a premeditated remark — said before any thought.

Beforethoughts

602   Almost everybody has afterthoughts. You have only before-thoughts.

TOLERANCE

Tolerant man

603   You're the most tolerant and forgiving man I know.
You just couldn't live with yourself if it were not so.

UNFAITHFULNESS

Been true

604   I must admit you've always been true. . .
But with that face, what else could you do?

VIOLENCE

Assault

605   I won't hit you — you aren't even worth your assault.

Whipping

606   I wish you the very best I can — a whipping.

Violence-prone

607   He's a violence-prone man. With his personality he's always being beaten up.

Kick heels

608   Somebody told me to kick my heels, but I was afraid you'd kick me back if I did.

Sense

609   It seems the only way you can have any sense put into you is to have it knocked out of you.

WAITER

Service

610   May I have some service? You're supposed to be the waiter, not me.

Dumbwaiter

611   We have a dumbwaiter like you in our apartment.

WEAKNESS

Cold shower

612 Every time danger threatens, he takes a cold shower — in his own sweat.

Brave

613 Nobody's as brave as you — not even you.

Courage

614 You have the courage to say what you believe — and it takes courage to give evidence that you're a fool.

Yellow streak

615 As he follows life's highway, he's guided by a yellow streak.

Chicken dinner

616 I'm not brave. If a cannibal ever eats me, he'll be having a chicken dinner.

WIT

Illumined by wit

617 Is our conversation to be illumined by the effulgence of your one-watt wit?

Half-witted

618 Not only are you half-witted — you picked the wrong half.

Game of wits

619 In any game of wits you don't need a handicap. Nature gave you that.

Wits' end

620 You're at your wits' end? I thought they ended long ago.

WRITING

Poetic license

621 In your case, poetic license should never have been issued.

Poetic justice

622 Hanging you for your verse would be poetic justice.

New records

623 My books have set new records for readership. More people than ever have not read them.

Moving play

624 It was a very moving play. Nobody could wait to leave.

Suspenseful book

625 It's a suspense book. You have to keep reading and reading to find out if there's ever going to be any good writing in it.

Depreciation

626 You should claim depreciation on your writing income. Your ability gets smaller every year.

Mark in world

627 He's really made his mark in the world of writing — but what else can one do when he doesn't know how to write?

Tearjerker

628 He wrote a tearjerker — so poor it makes you cry.

What you don't do

629 Like farmers, you should get paid for what you don't produce. In your case, that would be even better.

Part II
Boasts and Praises

Accolades
Actress
Aesthetics
Age
Angels
Audience
Beauty
Becoming
Best
Bikini
Binge
Birth
Blessings
Body
Bone Structure
Bowing
Boys
Brains
Brainstorm
Brilliance
Car
Charm
Children
Clothes
College
Compensation
Compliments
Conceit

Courage
Cream
Creator
Desirability
Destruction
Diamonds
Driver
Ecstasy
Environment
Evolution
Exile
Eyes
Face
Food
Friends
Frugality
Genealogy
Genes
Girls
Goodness
Greatness
Heart
Heaven
Holiness
Importance
Inebriation
Inimitable
Insults

Kissing
Knowledge
Light
Life
Lips
Looks
Love
Medicine
Mistake
Modesty
Money
Neurosis
Nirvana
Opinion
Optimism
Perception
Perfection
Pitches (for a date)
Pitches (for other things)
Pleasure
Proposals
Public

Public Service
Reflections
Religion
Repentance
Rightness
Single Status
Soul
Sports
Star
Status Symbol
Superiority
Talking
Thoughts
Tolerance
Truth
Unselfishness
Virtues
Voice
Wife
Wonderful
Writing

ACCOLADES
Red carpet

630 You should be called on the carpet — a red carpet.

What you are

631 You are what you are. You have my congratulations.

Nobody's perfect

632 To me you're a nobody. They say nobody's perfect.

Worthy of yourself

633 You've set your goals higher than any other man — you want to be worthy of yourself.

All by yourself

634 You're all by yourself — but that's plenty.

Even more so

635 The only thing wrong with the way you are is that you're not even more so.

Lean over backwards

636 He'll lean over backwards to achieve balance.

Struck it rich

637 It's every man for himself, and that means you struck it rich.

World owes

638 The world owes itself your living.

ACTRESS
Dramatic reading

639 You're such an actress, you could give a dramatic reading of the phone book.

Impossible

640 You're impossible! Nobody can be that good at acting.

Entertainer

641 I'm not in show business, but I'm an entertainer — I entertain everyone who meets me.

AESTHETICS
Fine arts

642 Fine Arts: Any you dabble in.

Aesthetic person

643   I'm an aesthetic person, but my looks are even more so.

Look good to them

644   Aesthetically inclined people make me sick. But they like me
      — I look good to them.

Mirror and frame

645   If you're an art lover and can't afford good paintings, just buy
      a fine mirror and frame it.

AGE

Don't age well

646   I don't age well. I never seem to get any older.

Getting older

647   You *are* getting older, but why do you try to hide it? You never
      look any older.

Years of heaven

648   Of course a young girl should marry an old man like me. Better
      a few years of heaven with me than many years of hell with some-
      body else.

ANGELS

All of the angels

649   I think you came into existence when all of the angels in heaven
      got together.

Doesn't believe

650   No one could look at you and say he doesn't believe in angels.

AUDIENCE

Audience with Pope

651   I was going to have an audience with the Pope, but when I offered
      to give him one he turned me down.

BEAUTY

Spoiled you

652   Your beauty has spoiled you. I want to despoil you.

Too beautiful for words

653   You're too beautiful for words — I won't argue with you.

My heavens

654 My heavens, but you're beautiful! I'm not being genteel in my profanity, just factual.

Don't despoil

655 Don't despoil our natural beauty. Don't be seen near me.

Sitting pretty

656 You're sitting pretty. You're pretty when you stand, too.

Has anyone told you?

657 Has anyone ever told you you're ugly? No, I didn't think so, because you're beautiful.

Wouldn't say

658 I wouldn't say you're good looking; I find beautiful women sometimes resent being told they are, so I'm not taking a chance with you.

Rich, young and beautiful

659 It's too bad you're not rich, young and beautiful — instead of being only young and beautiful.

Scenic tour

660 I'm going to take you on a scenic tour and show everyone the beauty that is you.

Straight in eyes

661 I can look you straight in the eyes and tell you they're beautiful.

Buff

662 I'm a beauty-in-the-buff buff.

BECOMING
Moonlight becomes you

663 Moonlight becomes you — but then, so does sunlight or any other kind.

BEST
Don't know any better

664 I must admit I think I'm great only because I don't know any better.

Beat you

665   I'd like to beat you, but you're better than I at everything.

As good as one can get

666   I seem to be about as good as one can get. What's more. . . ?

Success

667   I'm finally a success! It couldn't have happened to a nicer man.

Best man

668   You might say I'm not the best man who ever lived, but you'd be a liar if you did.

Feeling better

669   I'm feeling better now. But then, I always feel better than everyone.

Hadn't known me

670   When our founding forefathers wrote that "All men are created equal," they had only known kings, aristocrats, etc. — not me.

Better things in life

671   My wife married me because she wanted all the better things in life. Our problem was that after having acquired me, everything else had to be an anticlimax.

Hate myself

672   I hate myself for thinking I'm better than others. Why can't I have delusions like everybody else?

Don't blame you

673   I don't blame you for disliking me. Only your betters are a threat to you.

Haystack in a needle

674   Trying to find my equal is like looking for a haystack in a needle.

What is wrong?

675   Find what is wrong with this sentence: "I am the greatest man in the world" (Answer: It has a period missing.)

Equal opportunity

676   My company decided to give its employees an equal opportunity according to their skills. So they fired me — to give others a chance.

Look the best

677 I don't always look *my* best, but I always look *the* best.

The greatest

678 When people ask me, "How's everything?" I say, "The greatest!" (because I'm my everything).

BIKINI

Both see better

679 You should wear glasses and a bikini — then we can both see better.

BINGE

First-class binge

680 You're a first-class binge without the hangover.

Save my life

681 People are against my drinking liquor. They want to save my life, even if it kills me.

BIRTH

Long time

682 It took a long time to make me the genius I am — nine months

Lord repenteth

683 "And the Lord repenteth that he created man. . . " In atonement he gaveth the world me.

Born prematurely

684 I was born prematurely — I'm fifty years ahead of my time.

Harder to bear

685 I'll bet the only thing people find harder to bear than being themselves is their not being me.

Brilliant architects

686 If my parents planned me, they're brilliant architects.

Masterpiece

687 I'm such a masterpiece that my mother must have had to carry me longer than nine months.

Never been born

688 I wish you'd never been born — then I'd have something wonderful to look forward to.

BLESSINGS
Many blessings
689   I wish I could bestow as many blessings on you as nature has.

Don't give a damn
690   I don't give a damn for you — but blessings, yes.

BODY
Great body
691   I think the great body of mankind would agree that yours is the great body of mankind.

Escoffier
692   Nature was an Escoffier when it put together that dish.

Hip, hip
693   To a curvaceous girl: Hip, hip, hooray!

Nice girl
694   What's a nice girl like you doing in a place like your beautiful body?

Close to chest
695   She plays her cards close to her chest. In fact, they are her cards.

Physical characteristics
696   When I was young I thought all of my physical characteristics were the norm, that most men had them. Now I've learned they are the standard, that most men want them.

Nature cut corners
697   Nature certainly cut the corners when it made her! She's perfectly rounded.

Overdid a good thing
698   So what if I am fat — nature just overdid a good thing.

Never convince me
699   Science will never convince me that my body is mostly water. Water is too common.

BONE STRUCTURE
Beautiful bone structure
700   You have a beautiful bone structure. It holds you together and tears me apart.

BOWING
Turned knees

701 I turned my knees the other day. I was trying to bow to myself.

BOYS
Lowered their standards

702 Some boys aren't in love with me. They've just lowered their standards too high.

Secret of my success

703 The secret of my success with boys is that I make them feel important — I let them be seen with me.

I got my...

704 I got my bachelor's from Harvard, my doctor's from Columbia, and my married men from Yale.

BRAINS
Bad health

705 I have bad health because my brain uses so much blood there's not much left for the rest of my body.

Pretty bright

706 I'm a pretty bright person. In fact, I'd be pretty even if I were stupid — and I'd be stupid if I didn't think so.

Don't have my brains

707 Of course others don't think I'm as smart as I do — but then they don't have my brains to realize it.

Massive stroke

708 You know what a massive stroke is? That's the only kind that could affect my brain.

May be stupid

709 You may be very stupid, but I've got to give you credit for listening to intelligent people like you're doing right now.

Unabridged

710 I've got an unabridged brain.

Intelligent thing

711 The only intelligent thing you ever think about is me.

All of the brains

712 I think the Lord gave me all the brains he didn't give the world's fools to punish them for being stupid.

Obnoxious characteristic

713 I admit I'm afflicted with that most obnoxious characteristic — the ability to think.

So smart

714 If you're so smart, why aren't you rich instead of just brilliant?

Understatement

715 You think you're pretty smart, don't you? But you've always been given to understatement.

Brilliance

716 The only obstacle to my success is my brilliance and others' stupidity.

Sense and nonsense

717 Talking sense to me is like talking nonsense to anyone else. In both cases it's the way to convince.

Great riches

718 The great riches I claim to have are all in my head — my brains.

Humbling experience

719 The only humbling experience I've ever had is when I learned that I know more than anyone else. How could I have been so stupid as not to know it all along?

Electricity

720 People find me shocking because I have so much electricity coursing through my brain.

Be glad

721 You should be glad you aren't as brilliant as I. You don't have the brains to enjoy it.

Neither lead nor led

722 Neither do I lead nor am I led. People are too stupid to follow me, and I'm too bright to follow them.

No mind

723 I pay you no mind — my mind is too valuable.

BRAINSTORM

Brainstorming

724 I've found that when I have a brainstorming session with a group it's always productive — but only because I'm in it.

BRILLIANCE

Gossip

725 Of course I gossip. Genius will tell.

Obvious

726 I wouldn't say I'm a genius. Why state the obvious?

Safely assume

727 I think I can safely assume you're not brilliant. I'd be wrong, but you're powerless to stop me.

Hard time

728 You don't know how hard it is for me to be a genius — but then, you have a hard time holding on to your idiot status.

King of geniuses

729 Admittedly, I'm not the king of geniuses. I abdicated to give someone else a chance.

Poor fool

730 I'd make a poor fool, but I'm great as a genius.

Don't take credit

731 I don't take any credit for being brilliant. Actually, it's easy to be smart when you're a genius.

Debatable

732 I may not be a genius, but that's a debatable point.

No credit

733 People don't give me any credit for being a genius. They know it comes to me naturally.

After all

734 I've decided I'm not a genius after all. I'm a genius *before* all.

Mentally stable

735   I'm mentally stable — I stay at the genius level.

Community

736   I live in an intellectual community — my home.

Mind of my own

737   I have a mind of my own because I'm the only one worthy enough to own it.

Not long ago

738   It wasn't long ago that my genius was recognized by a great man. I guess I first realized it about ten years ago.

Bright direction

739   You should come to me for advice. That would be a step in the bright direction.

Motto

740   My motto is "Never admit to anything." But I don't always stick to it. I do admit I'm a genius.

You and I

741   You and I are brilliant people — me because I'm a genius, and you because you know I am.

CAR

Proud

742   I'm proud to be seen in my car because I'm in it.

Big cars

743   Talk about big cars! When I get in mine I'm so far away from people, I feel like a hermit.

Acres of hood

744   The thing I enjoy most about driving my new car is looking out over the acres and acres of hood and knowing they're all mine.

Delusions

745   If anyone ever stole my car, the police would soon nab him for felony and delusions of grandeur.

Wash job

746   I'm buying another car because my old one needs a wash job.

CHARM
Charming
747 There's something about you I find particularly charming. The trouble is, I'm not always around you.

Eureka
748 One time I was wondering about great charm. Suddenly I yelled, "Eureka, I have it!"

Homewrecking
749 With your charm you should go into the homewrecking business.

Entertaining way
750 Charm: The ability to say nothing in an entertaining way.

CHILDREN
Obnoxious
751 Even if I were an obnoxious child it would have been worth it, considering what I am today.

Problem children
752 We were both problem children, you at creating them and me at solving them.

You're good
753 You're good with kids. You're good without them, too.

Quality
754 I'd like to improve the quality of human life, but I don't see how I can father all of the children.

Darling
755 Women treat me as though I were still a baby. They thought I was the darlingest thing in the world then, too.

Take after
756 It's because my kids don't take after me that I have to take after them.

Extraordinary
757 My kids are nothing out of the ordinary — they came out of the extraordinary.

CLOTHES

Sartorialist

758   Am I a superb sartorialist? When they want to decorate Main Street, they have me stand on the corner.

Pretty dress

759   I like that pretty dress you're wearing. Can I talk you out of it?

Best-dressed

760   You're the best-dressed man in town when I'm on your arm. They won't name him best-dressed man of the year again after I stop giving him my clothes.

Most fashionable

761   I wear the most fashionable clothes; that's what they become when I'm seen in them.

COLLEGE

Too smart

762   "He couldn't make it in college."
"Too dumb?"
"No, too smart."

I'm a teacher

763   I'm a teacher. Not in a school — through example and wisdom.

Wasted life

764   Mine has been a wasted and profligate life. I've expended immense sums of genius in vainly trying to enlighten people.

ABC's

765   "You've forgotten your ABC's?"
"Yes, because I never get anything except A's."

COMPENSATION

God's compensation

766   She is God's compensation for having made others.

COMPLIMENTS

Smooth

767   Your hands are as smooth as a woman telling a man why he should get married.

Compliment without danger

768 Compliment to pay a girl without endangering your bachelor's bliss: Your teeth are as white as a man's face when he first sees his wife in pin curlers.

Groom's head

769 Your skin is as soft as a groom's head.

Illusions

770 Your face is as beautiful as the illusions of two people in love.

Perfume

771 With that perfume you're wearing, you can lead men around by their noses.

Combat

772 You're an expert in mouth to ear combat.

Suppose that your girl friend has just accused you of never paying her any compliments. You defend yourself:

Stand in line

773 I'd stand in line to give you one!

Dope

774 You're sure a dope — and am I ever addicted to you!

Right mind

775 No man in his right mind could associate with you. Your beauty drives all men mad.

Functional

776 Are you functional as well as ornamental?

Crush on you

777 I've got a crush on you — but I'd like a tighter one.

Suppose that you wish to compliment both yourself and your date at the same time. Here's how:

No trouble

778 Do you have exquisite taste, perspicacity and intelligence? Good! Then I'll have no trouble winning your heart.

Desirable

779 You have all that's desirable for a woman — me.

Worthy

780 What greater compliment can I pay a girl than to say, "You are worthy of my aspirations"?

Lucky girl

781 How much do I think of you? You've got me, you lucky girl!

CONCEIT

Suppose that someone has accused you of an inordinate fondness for yourself. You agree:

Can't beat me

782 So I boast. At least I encourage others to do the same — I know they can't beat me at it.

Seeing reality

783 My egotism doesn't keep me from seeing reality. In fact, it's my seeing reality that made me egotistical.

Something in common

784 You're as conceited as I am. But then it's nice to have something in common with me, even if it's only conceit.

Worthwhile

785 Boasts are worthwhile. Everyone can't be the best, but everyone can talk as though he is.

Suit yourself

786 When people say to me, "Suit yourself," I reply, "I suit myself just fine."

Inverse ratio

787 There is an inverse ratio between worth and braggadocio. That's why I'm modest.

Powers of description

788 I don't like to insult or brag, but powers of description are my forte.

Never tire

789 It's true, I never tire of anywhere I am.

Build up

790 I build myself up with vitamins and boasting.

COURAGE
Brave
791 Brave? Listen, I'm a regular dare-do-well.

Tough
792 Tough? Listen, the only reason I don't call out the Marines is that even they're afraid to come against me.

CREAM
Whipped cream
793 The reason life has been so hard on me is that people like whipped cream.

Butterfat
794 My overweight isn't lard. I'm cream, and I have a lot of butter-fat.

CREATOR
Precocious child
795 I was a precocious child. When only twelve I asked my mother, "Is God made in my image?"

Play God
796 I never play God. Who acts?

Superb job
797 I worship my maker. He did a superb job!

DESIRABILITY
Robbing the cradle
798 You're robbing the cradle — you're not getting married.

Homely women
799 I really feel sorry for homely women — none of them can ever get me.

Broad shoulders
800 He has broad shoulders. There's always one on them.

Unlucky
801 Women are unlucky in love; the vast majority haven't met me.

Miraculous
802 It doesn't strike me as being miraculous when a woman falls in love with me — only when she doesn't.

Sorry for women

803 Despite how I criticize them, I do feel sorry for women. Only one can have me as a husband.

Don't complain

804 Don't complain about your marriage. If the Lord had wanted you to be happily married, he'd have given you me as a spouse.

Unusual girl

805 I must admit it takes an unusual girl to prefer me to other men. She has to be one who prefers brains to ignorance, good looks to plainness, character to depravity, etc.

Shooting

806 I'm something worth shooting for — you're something worth shooting at.

Would buy

807 Let's put it this way: If all wealthy fathers wanted to buy their daughters a husband for a wedding present, I'm what they'd buy.

Convention of girls

808 I was going to hold a convention of my girls, but I couldn't find a convention hall big enough.

Winning hand

809 You're holding the winning hand — mine.

Everything

810 For the girl who has everything — me.

Day is complete

811 When a girl meets me, her day is complete. When one meets you, her day is completed.

Formality

812 When I proposition a girl, I let her go through the formality of saying "Yes" before I congratulate her.

Looking at you

813 I've just been looking at you. Please permit me to say — Wow!

Responsibility

814 I don't like the responsibility of having so many women's happiness on my shoulders.

DESTRUCTION
No reason for saving

815 The day I die is when the world will come to an end, because there'll no longer be any reason for saving it.

DIAMONDS
Gild the lily

816 For you to wear diamonds is to gild the lily.

Paradox

817 Your words are a paradox. They're abundant as rocks and yet as precious as diamonds.

DRIVER
Notches

818 These aren't scratches on the side of my car — they're notches!

ECSTASY
Everest

819 You're the Everest of ecstasy.

Enjoy looking

820 I'm glad I can't see through you. I enjoy looking at you too much.

New encyclical

821 If you keep looking that attractive, the Pope will have to put out a new encyclical.

Orgy

822 One look at you is an orgy.

ENVIRONMENT
Part of it

823 I always like my environment because I'm part of it.

EVOLUTION
Not in vain

824 Every time I look at myself I think how wonderful it is that all of these millions of years of evolution haven't been in vain.

Evolution stopped

825 Evolution stopped with you. You can't be improved.

Working toward

826 I believe in evolution. After all, I'm what it has been working toward.

EXILE

Foreign policy

827 The government was going to exile me, but then it decided that improving its foreign policy wasn't that important.

EYES

Only have eyes

828 I only have eyes for you — no money or anything else.

Eye-witness

829 I'm an eye-witness, and I can testify that yours are beautiful.

FACE

Never lose face

830 I hope you never lose face. One like that belongs to the world.

Tattoo

831 Let me tattoo my picture on your face so I can stare at two things I love.

Hide your face

832 Why don't you go hide your face — stop spoiling people!

Confrontation

833 In any face-to-face confrontation, you'd win. Yours would always be prettier.

Poker face

834 You've got a poker face — it has stirred up a lot of fire.

Generous face

835 You have a generous face — it's always giving joy to those who look at it.

Face value

836 If I were accepted at face value, I'd be rich.

Best face

837 She always puts her best face forward.

Blemish

838 If a blemish were ever to appear on your face, I wouldn't think, "Unfortunate you," I'd think, "Fortunate blemish."

FOOD

Thorough fare

839 After eating dinner: That was a thorough fare — you left nothing out.

First in line

840 Anyone who isn't first in line to eat my food shouldn't get any, because he didn't appreciate it enough to be first.

Good bread

841 This is marvelous bread you made! I call it the miracle of the loaves.

Desserter

842 This confection is going to turn me into a desserter!

FRIENDS

No poor friends

843 I don't have any poor friends. Anyone having me as a friend is rich.

FRUGALITY

Dime in bank

844 Talk about frugality! He's put a dime in the bank for every dollar he spends — but it's always the same dime.

GENEALOGY

Resent the fact

845 I resent the fact you didn't have to work or make any sacrifice to get me as a relative.

Not interested

846 I'm not interested in genealogy. No matter how great my antecedents, they were only leading up to me, the ultimate.

GENES

Unborn children

847 If you love your unborn children, you'll give them my genes.

Abhorrence

848 Nature imbued me with an abhorrence for ugly and stupid women. This keeps me from polluting my perfect genes.

Superior love

849 You must be endowed with a superior parental love — you love the kids who carry your genes.

Give the world

850 I wish I could give the world my genes without having babies.

GIRLS

Inferior

851 They make me feel inferior — to think I'd want anything to do with them.

Hold their distance

852 Goodlooking girls should hold my hands — all others, their distance.

Won't stand

853 I won't stand for any girl but you. I sit for all the others.

Not bad

854 Girly, you're not bad. Too bad!

Eve

855 If you had been Eve, Adam wouldn't have lost the Garden of Eden — he'd have taken it with him.

Mechanically inclined

856 She's one girl who's mechanically inclined. Ever since she had to pay a bill for car repairs she's been after a mechanic.

Free passes

857 She likes to go out with boys because they give her lots of free passes.

Fishing

858 My daughter went fishing and did very well — she landed one fish and ten fishermen.

Never had a thought

859 It's funny how a woman who's never had a thought in her life can give men all kinds of ideas.

The real me

860 I need a girl who has the ability to see beneath my good looks, charm and brains, and love the real me — for my character.

Pass away

861 If you think you're going to flirt with me, all I can say is, "Pass away!"

Far beyond

862 I'm surprised when women try to catch me, because I'm so far beyond anything they could logically dream of getting.

GOODNESS

Self-righteous

863 I'm self-righteous. I certainly haven't been able to make anyone else righteous.

Wise guy

864 When people call me a wise guy, that's no term of disapproval — it's a sign of recognition.

Right with America

865 We need to talk more about what is right with America — but I really shouldn't be the subject of every conversation.

Too righteous

866 I am far too righteous to ever be sanctimonious.

Good thing

867 It's a good thing you're a good thing.

Decent

868 There's something decent about you — me.

Courage

869 I've always had the courage to know the world is evil — and I'm not.

All right

870 I'm all right. In fact, I'm superb.

Goodness me

871 Goodness me, but goodness is me.

Going to apologize

872   The last time I was selfish I was going to apologize, but I hadn't
      yet learned to talk then.

Pretty good

873   You're not pretty good, you're beautifully good.

My goodness

874   When I say "My goodness," I mean it!

Up to

875   What am I up to? Anybody or anything.

Temptation

876   I never yield to temptation. I've never once gotten out of its
      way.

More honest

877   You're more honest than I. Not one of your many lies has
      been as big as this one.

Primrose

878   She's my virtuous flower — sort of a primrose.

Injustice

879   It is for me to cry out against injustice, and it is for the rest
      of the world to perpetuate it.

Self-realization

880   I'm striving for self-realization. I don't yet realize how good I
      am.

Bad-good

881   She is bad, and that is good.

GREATNESS

Greater than myself

882   I'm willing to give my life for any cause greater than myself.
      Fortunately, there is none.

Multiple personalities

883   I'm the ten greatest men.

Rock of Ages

884   I'm like the song "Rock of Ages" — I'm a magnificent him.

Feeling great

885 I'm feeling great — but let's face it, I am great.

Beside myself

886 Sometimes I feel I'm not far from greatness, but that's only when I'm beside myself.

Greatest fool

887 If I'm a fool, I'm the world's *greatest* fool.

HEART

After my own heart

888 You're a girl after my own heart — and you may get it yet.

Best heart

889 I have the best heart in the world. It's keeping me alive.

HEAVEN

In touch with heaven

890 To girl whose hand you're holding: I'm in touch with heaven.

Wonderful place

891 I'll find heaven a wonderful place because I'll be there.

Ironic

892 It's ironic that I, with the most to gain from heaven, am the one who doesn't believe in its existence.

Truly heaven

893 In the next life we'll be judged for what we are. That being the case, for me it will truly be heaven.

Called down

894 I'm so happy that you were called down from heaven! I couldn't have gotten along without you.

Good works

895 I take full credit for my good works and for publicizing them. This will keep me from getting a reward in heaven, but I'm not doing my good works for any selfish reasons.

Not good enough

896 I'll never go to heaven — it's not good enough for me.

HOLINESS

His Holiness
897 People call me His Holiness and you His Homeliness.

Kiss my feet
898 I tell the women I'll kiss their hands if they'll kiss my feet.

Holy ground
899 Nobody can refuse me burial in holy ground — any place I'm buried will be holy.

Great respect
900 I treat you with great respect, as though you're my peer.

Don't have me
901 I don't blame superstitious savages for their benighted ways. After all, they don't have me to set them straight.

To save his soul
902 He can't believe what I tell him to save his soul — and that's what it will take to save his soul.

Not a god
903 I realize I'm not a god. Otherwise I could convince people of anything, including that fact.

Penny
904 Here, have a penny untouched by human hands.

Godly man
905 I'm not a godly man. I prefer being godlike.

Sensitive person
906 I'm not a sensitive person, but when someone says, "Oh, my God!" I take it personally.

IMPORTANCE

Copernicus
907 Copernicus was wrong as far as I'm concerned. *You're* the center of the solar system.

Not available
908 No girl can have everything — I'm not available.

Hold everything

909 Hold everything — then squeeze me!

Thinking about

910 What am I thinking about? Oh, everything — to wit, myself.

Something trivial

911 Are you talking about something trivial, or are you discussing me?

Main thing

912 The main thing — is me.

Pedestal

913 I want a wife who'll keep me in my place — on a pedestal.

INEBRIATION

See double

914 Looking at you is enough to make me want to go out and get drunk, so I can see double.

INIMITABLE

World needs more

915 I'm inimitable. More's the pity, since the world needs more like me.

INSULTS

Not imaginative enough

916 They say women like to be insulted, but I'm not imaginative enough to think of one for you.

Precious stone

917 I criticize you for your own good — any stone I throw at you is a precious one.

Be complimented

918 You should be complimented if I stop bragging about myself long enough to insult you.

KISSING

Kissing sickness

919 He has the kissing sickness. That's all he makes girls want to do.

Boomerang

920   When I throw a kiss, it's with a boomerang.

KNOWLEDGE
More than you know

921   More than you know — I do.

Little knowledge

922   They say a little knowledge is a dangerous thing, but you and I are safe — I from having a lot of knowledge, and you from having none.

Fear of the unknown

923   I have a fear of the unknown. Maybe that's why I've learned everything.

All the answers

924   I have all the answers. Now if I only knew the proper questions.

Smithsonian

925   When I read that the Smithsonian Institution was founded for the increase and diffusion of knowledge among men, I thought they were talking about you.

LIGHT
Blows a fuse

926   If my mind ever blows a fuse, it will be from giving too much light.

Let there be light

927   And God said, "Let there be light." But I wasn't born for some time after.

LIFE
I regret

928   I regret that this is the only life I'll ever have. At least it's better than anyone else will ever have.

LIPS
Lip service

929   I'd like to pay you some lip service.

Smack you

930 I'd like to smack you — right on the lips.

Lip reader

931 I'm a lip reader, and I read yours as saying, "I want to be kissed."

LOOKS

Gorgeous

932 Men think I'm gorgeous, but that's only because they don't know how good-looking I really am.

Aphrodisiac

933 Thank you for the aphrodisiac — looking at you.

People lie

934 People lie about his looks and tell him he's handsome. They lie about mine, too — they tell me I'm ugly.

Blind man

935 A blind man could see you're ugly — but anyone with eyes knows you're beautiful.

Watch your step

936 Watch your step — I'm watching the rest of you.

If looks were money

937 If good looks were money, I'd hate to have to pay your taxes.

Gift

938 Well, I see you brought me a gift — your good looks.

Good look

939 He took a good look at her. Of course, any look at her is good.

Humble you

940 Doesn't it humble you to think there may be a better looking girl in the world?

LOVE

Love at first slight

941 You've been so successful with men that I think it could be love at first slight.

Virtue

942 The only virtue you lack is being in love with me.

Gave you a home

943 I gave you a home within my heart,
A home from which you'll never part;
For the laws of love are very strict,
And try as I will, I can't evict
A tenacious tenant, a reprobate
Who won't pay the rent, yet won't vacate.

Worthy of me

944 Everyone needs someone other than himself to love. Oh, if
only someone else were worthy of me!

Worth loving

945 I love you because anyone that a man like me would love has
to be worth loving.

Love of a good man

946 Why do I need the love of a good woman when I already have
the love of a good man?

Love me?

947 How do I love me? Every woman enjoys the love of a good
man, and so do I.

Nine lives

948 I wish you had nine lives so I could love every one of them.

Love affair

949 Ours is a seven-alarm love affair.

Mutual love

950 When a girl falls in love with me it's a case of mutual love
even though I hate her.

Good taste

951 I'm the type of person with whom only people with impeccable
good taste fall in love. That's why I'm the only one who loves
me.

Noble love

952 How can you say that his love for himself is anything but
noble? It's the only love in the world that's constant and true!

Too choosy

953 I don't like girls who are too choosy. Other men need to be loved, too.

Love beyond all else

954 I thought I'd like to put my heart into something I love beyond all else — but then I realized it already is.

Love letter

955 Love letter: I.

MEDICINE

Bitter man

956 Maybe I am a bitter man — medicines usually are.

New man

957 The doctor gave me some medicine that makes me feel like a new man, and I resent it. Being anything other than what I am is inferior.

Painful sore

958 I've got a painful sore. This astounds me. I didn't think a sore of mine would hurt me.

MISTAKE

First to admit

959 I'm the first to admit mistakes — yours in particular.

Don't care

960 I don't care if I do make a mistake. I like to experience everything.

Only man alive

961 I'm the only man alive who doesn't blame his faults on others — 'cause I haven't got any.

Stupidity

962 I was fired for stupidity — theirs, not mine.

Same mistake once

963 I'm the type who never makes the same mistake once.

Hate myself

964 There are times when I hate myself — those times when I feel I've sinned. How could I ever think anything so foolish?

MODESTY

Modesty

965 Modesty: My immodesty in others.

Bragging

966 My so-called bragging is really a form of modesty, since I never say I'm as good as I really am.

Humility

967 So I don't have any humility — that's the only virtue I don't have.

Humbleness

968 Humbleness doesn't become me. I've nothing to be humble about.

Not conceited

969 I'm not conceited enough to think I'm not conceited.

At his feet

970 He never picks up anything he drops. He thinks he's the only person who shouldn't be at his feet.

Arrogant

971 It's true I'm arrogant, but it's a humble arrogance — not nearly as much as my worth deserves.

Good enough?

972 Every now and then she does have humility. She wonders if she's good enough to deserve herself.

No right

973 I hate people who are as conceited as I am. No one else has a right to be.

Americans

974 I'm not one of those conceited people who think they're great because they're Americans. I think America is great because I'm an American!

MONEY

Pin money

975 I sold some stock to give my wife some pin money, and the Dow Jones average dropped twenty points.

Self-made man

976 I'm a self-made man who could earn a fortune if I went into the construction business.

Blessings

977 Ordinarily, money, good looks, intelligence, good personality and all other blessings go together, but you don't have money.

Earn much money?

978 Does he earn much money? Let's just say that if his taxes were raised 1 percent, everyone else's could be lowered 99 percent.

NEUROSIS
Psychiatrist

979 I'd go to a psychiatrist, but I don't really think I could help him.

Adjusted

980 I'm normal — I've adjusted to my neuroses.

NIRVANA
Nirvana

981 To me, Nirvana is becoming as good as I think I am.

OPINION
Superb taste

982 If you want my opinion. . . you've got superb taste.

Well informed

983 His opinions are as well informed as they are well formed.

Prejudiced

984 Yes, I'm prejudiced — by the facts.

My opinions

985 Your opinions are what others believe. My opinions are what others will come to believe.

Never sure

986 I'm never sure of an opinion until I state it.

Two sides

987 There are two sides to every argument — my side and the wrong side.

OPTIMISM
Positively
988 I'm positively negative.

Incurable optimist
989 Who dares say I'm not an incurable optimist when my goal is to make people as good as I!

PERCEPTION
Don't resent
990 I don't resent anyone who points out my mistakes. Anyone so singularly perspicacious is laudatory.

PERFECTION
Not all bad
991 You're not all bad and I'm not all perfect — you're just bad and I'm just perfect.

Individual
992 You shouldn't want everyone to be perfect. Don't you like being an individual?

Really something
993 Nothing's perfect — but you're really something.

Inventive
994 He's so inventive, the only thing he can't figure out how to improve is himself.

Bad as can be
995 She's as bad as she can possibly be, but it's impossible for her to be less than perfect.

Shameless
996 I'm shameless — I've never done anything to be ashamed of.

Perfectability
997 I believe in the ultimate perfectability of man, because you're proof of it.

One-way street
998 Life is a one-way street — my way.

Many things

999 There are many things I don't like about myself, and you're one of them.

Obnoxious

1000 I apologize! I know I've been obnoxious. There's nothing more revolting than a person who not only thinks he's always right, but *is* always right.

Less than perfect

1001 Don't let it bother you that you're less than perfect. You're hardly the only person inferior to me.

Only thing wrong

1002 The only thing wrong with the way you are is that you're not even more so.

Disenchantment

1003 Of course my disenchantment with people is greater than anyone else's. After all, we compare others to ourselves.

Just perfect

1004 Someone told her, "You're just perfect," and she said, "Is that all?"

Don't you know better?

1005 Don't you know better than to argue with me? If you knew better, you'd know I'm right.

What's wrong

1006 I'd like to know what's wrong with you. I certainly can't see anything.

The trouble

1007 The trouble with being perfect is that it leaves nothing for me to aspire to.

Lost

1008 I was wandering lost through the forests of life, looking for perfection. Lo and behold, one day I found I had already passed it.

Bad boy

1009   I must confess I've been a bad boy, but I'm perfect as a man.

Advanced beyond

1010   Perfection is something he has advanced beyond. He now has frailties.

More like you

1011   You think you're perfect? That makes me more like you than you are.

Nobody's perfect

1012   Nobody's perfect — but I'm a somebody.

Tired

1013   Do you find life wearisome — tired of always being right?

PITCHES (for a date)

Worth pursuing

1014   The only subject worth pursuing is you.

Fancy

1015   Well, fancy meeting you — and I do!

Sprightly as an elf

1016   My soul would be sprightly as an elf
If I were beside you instead of myself.

Familiar

1017   You look familiar — and you look as though you want to be.

Get in trouble

1018   Why don't you get in trouble, damsel, so I can rescue you?

Least resistance

1019   I'm trying to find the line of least resistance.

Good enough to eat

1020   You look good enough to eat, so let me take you to supper.

Special interests

1021   Ordinarily I don't like special interests, but I'd like to be yours.

Lost my head

1022   You make me feel like John the Baptist — I've lost my head over you.

Ache

1023   You give me a pain — I ache for you.

Food supplement

1024   You're my food supplement. Man cannot live by bread alone.

PITCHES (for other things)
Good impression

1025   To girl: Leave a good impression on me.

Civil liberties

1026   I believe in civil liberties, but I'd like to take some uncivil liberties with you.

Together

1027   Let's pull ourselves together. We've been apart long enough.

Back to fold

1028   Welcome back to the fold! Let me enfold you.

Kissoff

1029   Let's not have a kissoff without a kiss.

Smack

1030   If you give me a smack on one cheek, I'll turn the other.

Grips

1031   To good-looking girl: Let's come to grips.

Holdings

1032   I'd like to add you to my holdings.

One problem

1033   You're one problem I'd like to grasp.

Restrained

1034   Your beauty drives me mad! Put your arms around me to restrain me.

Squeeze you

1035   You affect me like an empty tube of toothpaste — I want to squeeze you dry.

Roman

1036   I'm no Roman, but seeing you makes me want to be a seizer.

PLEASURE
Part of the time
1037   A good part of the time I'm around people, and a bad part of the time you are.

All yours
1038   So we meet again! Let me assure you the pleasure's all yours.

PROPOSALS
Entitled
1039   I'm entitled to you. You're my divine right.

Love is true
1040   Dear girl, my love is perfect and true;
I'll even take your mother along with you.

Have a heart
1041   Have a heart! Give mine back to me.

Give me
1042   Give me your ear — and your heart.

Opportunity
1043   Every girl should have the opportunity to turn down the world's most eligible bachelor. So will you marry me?

PUBLIC
Grateful public
1044   I'm my public, and a grateful one.

PUBLIC SERVICE
Walk down street
1045   To beautiful girl: Why don't you walk down the street, as a public service?

REFLECTIONS
Two mirrors
1046   She uses two mirrors so she can look at her reflection endlessly.

RELIGION
Sanctimonious
1047   He's a truly sanctimonious man who thinks he has everything to die for.

Suppose that you have been accused of being irreligious. Defend youself with:

Superior being

1048 There was a time when I felt close to a superior being. Then I found I was beside myself.

Nobody came

1049 The Christian Association called a mass meeting of all men of good will. But nobody came — I was ill.

Many blessings

1050 I do count my many blessings, but people call me conceited.

Reincarnation

1051 I believe in reincarnation. It would take more than one life to make somebody so perfect.

The gospel

1052 I tell only the gospel because anything I say is the gospel.

Suppose that some self-righteous person has thundered that you will be punished for your sins. You respond (if you get a chance) with one or more of the following:

Love sinners

1053 God must love sinners more than the righteous, because he made more of them.

Hell

1054 Hell's not a bad place to be. *I'll* be there.

REPENTANCE
Wonderful thing

1055 I believe repentance is such a wonderful thing that I wish I had some need for it.

RIGHTNESS
All right

1056 Everything is all right with me. In fact, everything about me is superb.

Disagree

1057 When someone tells me he has to disagree with me, I say, "I

should hope you have to. You should have better sense than
to do it voluntarily."

SINGLE STATUS

Spoiling women
1058 I don't believe in spoiling women. That's why I don't get married.

Higher things
1059 Most women aspire to higher things, but so far none has caught
me.

High opinion
1060 To think she could get him as a husband is to have an inor-
dinately high opinion of herself and a low one of him.

Fortunate man
1061 I'd be the most fortunate man in the world if I had a girl who
deserves me.

Little pride
1062 The other day a beautiful, talented, wealthy girl proposed to
me. I don't understand it. How could a girl with so little pride
as to propose to a man be so conceited as to think she's worthy
of me?

Girl watcher
1063 He's an ardent girl watcher — he watches them carefully to
make sure one doesn't get him.

Come-uppance
1064 He receives a come-uppance from a lot of girls. All of them
tell him to come up to their places.

Can't wed
1065 I can't wed. If I married one girl, then in fairness I'd have to
marry them all.

Telephone
1066 I don't want a telephone because I'm afraid girls will get my
number.

SOUL

Fancy raiment
1067 You're one person who doesn't need to spend money on fancy
raiment. Just dress yourself in your soul.

SPORTS
Poker
1068 I'm so good at poker we save time by cutting cards to see who will give me his money first, because the only element of chance is how much they'll lose.

Skiing
1069 I ski so fast that I make the snow melt, thus letting me water-ski down a mountainside.

STAR
Astronomy
1070 I'm studying astronomy so I can find out if there was a new star in the sky the night I was born.

STATUS SYMBOL
Favorite symbol
1071 My favorite status symbol is my face.

Award
1072 I just won the Man of the Year Award sponsored by the (your name) Foundation.

SUPERIORITY
Population increase
1073 You should like seeing the population increase, because that means you are superior to more people.

Superior to
1074 God made you so everyone else would have someone to be superior to. He made everyone else so I'd have someone to feel superior to.

Hold a candle
1075 Nobody can hold a candle to me, although plenty of people would like to.

Complex
1076 They say nobody's perfect. Mine isn't a simple superiority complex — it's a complex complex.

Best there is
1077 I don't enjoy being superior. After all, if I'm the best there is, what hope is there for the world?

Stupid

1078   Sometimes I act pretty stupid, just so people will accept me as an equal.

Delusions

1079   In my youth I had delusions of mediocrity, but finally I faced reality.

Up to

1080   Whatever you're up to, you'll never be up to me.

Top of pile

1081   When it comes to people,
I'm at the top of the pile.
But you're only a part
Of the rank and vile.

Acquaintance with me

1082   Does your acquaintance with me make you feel inferior by contrast or superior for knowing me?

All I ask

1083   All I ask is that people let me be myself. One can't ask for more than that.

All in mind

1084   My vaunted superiority to other people is all in my mind. That's how I excel, with my mind.

The best

1085   Everything else being equal, I'd still be the best.

Beat all

1086   Well, if I don't beat all!

Comedown

1087   I'd like to believe I'm as good as other people, but I can't. Too much of a comedown.

TALKING

Anything worthwhile

1088   I listen to anyone who has anything worthwhile to say. That's why I do all the talking.

Public service

1089 I'll now associate with you, as a non-profit public service.

Smarter than I

1090 Don't ask me what I'm saying. You're smarter than I, so if you don't know what I'm talking about, how should I?

No self-control

1091 I make enemies because I just have no self-control around people. I compulsively talk sense to them.

Gab

1092 Please give me the gift of your gab.

Important

1093 After people listen to me they always feel more important. After all, *I* spoke to them.

THOUGHTS

Original thinker

1094 If you want to be a truly original thinker, let me do your thinking for you.

Think of next

1095 What won't they think of next? Something I haven't already thought of.

Very idea

1096 The very idea! That's what I've had.

Pleasant thought

1097 I just had a pleasant thought! I was thinking about you.

Meeting of minds

1098 Let's have a meeting of the minds. I'll put mine on the elevator and press the down button.

Reflections

1099 He sparkles forth ideas like reflections from the facets of a diamond.

Deep thoughts

1100 He's deep in thought — in fact, his thoughts are always deep.

TOLERANCE
More tolerant
1101 I must admit you're more tolerant of me than I am of you — but then you have less to be tolerant about.

Disappointed in others
1102 Of course you're more tolerant of others' faults than I. It's only when you're perfect that you can be disappointed in others.

Make mistakes
1103 I do make mistakes. I've been too tolerant of those who disagree with me.

Demand
1104 I demand that you be as tolerant as I!

TRUTH
Don't like truth
1105 People never like to hear the truth. They get just as angry when I tell them they're inferior as they do when I tell them I'm superior.

Believe everything
1106 I believe everything I hear because I won't listen to anything except the truth.

Good principle
1107 Here's a good principle to use in deciding what is truth: If I don't tell it to you, don't believe it.

Penalty
1108 He's accustomed to not being believed. That's the penalty for telling the truth.

Hate myself
1109 Sometimes I hate myself because even I can turn against truth.

Rare people
1110 I'm one of those rare people who want to hear the truth about themselves no matter what it is. I enjoy receiving compliments.

Gospel truth
1111 You're supposed to accept everything I say as the gospel truth — until I change my mind.

How do you know?

1112 How do you know that's true? I didn't tell it to you.

Lie a lot

1113 I lie a lot. Believe me.

UNSELFISHNESS
Essence of unselfishness

1114 I consider my admitted selfishness to be the essence of un-selfishness, because the good care I take of myself assures that nobody else will have to.

VIRTUES
Always right

1115 Except when I'm wrong, I'm always right.

Better

1116 'Twere better you had my vices than your virtues.

All genuine

1117 The only thing artificial about me is my faults. My virtues are all genuine.

VOICE
Sound system

1118 What a voice! You're a great sound system.

Records

1119 If we went into the record business, with my voice there would be a lot of records broken. In your case they'd be set.

WIFE
Agreeable wife

1120 I want an agreeable wife — one who agrees I'm as good as I think I am.

Can't improve

1121 My wife said she doesn't know what to make of me, and I told her she just can't improve on what I am.

Loved herself

1122 I thought I'd found a wife who loved me as much as I love me. Unfortunately, I learned she loved herself as much as I love me.

Doesn't appreciate

1123   I've given my wife everything, but she doesn't appreciate me.

Truth

1124   Truth is like my wife: sought by others, desirable, but known only by me.

Pitiable

1125   She's pitiable because she can't land me as a mate, but even more pitiable because she doesn't want to.

To my wife on her anniversary:

1126   I like washing machines, waxing machines,
automatic dishwashers, and refrigerators,
but you're my very favorite labor saver.

WONDERFUL

Compliment

1127   I don't know who is luckiest — you for being so wonderful or me for knowing you.

WRITING

Great American Novel

1128   The Great American Novel has never been written. I haven't started it yet.

Fine print

1129   You'd do well to read the fine print in my books. All of it is fine — just grand, in fact.

Like most

1130   The thing I like most about having a book published is that now I personally know an author!

Part III
Witticisms, Wisecracks and Comebacks

Alcohol
Alimony
Appearance
Astronauts
Automobiles
Babies
Bachelor
Bikini
Bills
Capital Punishment
Censors
Clothes
Complainers
Courtship
Cynics
Dating (and Related
    Activities)
Divorce
Doctors
Dogs
Earthquake
Eating
Epitaphs
Excuses
Finance
Florida
Friend
Funerals

Gambling
Girls
Gossip
Government
Health
Henpecking
Husbands
Indians
Jobs
Judges
Kids
Law
Lawyers
Lazy Relatives
Liars
Life
Love
Marijuana
Marriage
Miscellaneous
Money
Movies
Not-So-Nutty Notions
Nudity
Overweight
Painting
Parking
Philosophy

Race Prejudice
Rape
Rejections
Sex
Silly Syllogisms
Smoking
Taxes
Tears
Telephone
Television

Truth
Unisex Styles
War
Weddings
Wisdom
Wives
Women
Work
Youth

ALCOHOL

Alcoholic's cry

1131   The alcoholic's cry: My head's not high,
                                But, boy, am I!

Inebriation

1132   Inebriation: That state at which the drinker thinks he likes
        the taste of alcohol.

Cry in beer

1133   I cry in my beer. I don't like beer.

Night clubs

1134   Night clubs smash people.

Sobering up

1135   Sobering up: unloading.

Dr. Jekyll

1136   Dr. Jekyll wasn't so hot. A chemical that turns man into a Mr.
        Hyde has been known for centuries. It's called alcohol.

Lush

1137   Lush — one who's overloaded.

High and dry

1138   In the lush's lexicon, "high and dry" is a contradiction in terms.

Drink to that

1139   "You're an alcoholic!"
        "I'll drink to that."

High dive

1140   High dive: an expensive saloon.

Handle liquor

1141   I know how to handle my liquor — gingerly.

With every breath

1142   You advertise you're an alcoholic with every breath.

Drowns in alcohol

1143   The man who drowns himself in alcohol is usually trying to
        hold his head above water.

Tight ship

1144   That captain runs a tight ship. His crew is always drunk.

Everyone wondering

1145   My girl never swears or drinks, and everyone wonders why she isn't ladylike.

Drinking and driving slogans

1146   If you're driven to drink, don't drive yourself from it.

A man would have to be drunk to drive a car while drunk.

If you mix your drinking and driving, you'll be having a car upon the rocks.

The easiest way a woman can drive a man to drink is for her to drive the car — even if he isn't in it.

ALIMONY

Gambling debt

1147   Alimony: gambling debt

Aid and comfort

1148   Alimony: aid and comfort to the enemy.

Slipknot

1149   When she ties the knot with her men, she makes sure it's a slipknot.

Rank discrimination

1150   We practice rank discrimination against women. We'll only let them collect alimony from one man at a time, but we'll let a man pay it to more than one woman at a time.

More and more

1151   More and more women are making successes of their marriages. Alimony payments are going up.

Lifelike doll

1152   I'm going to invent a doll that is so lifelike it cries, laughs and collects alimony.

Keep collecting

1153   A wife is the only landlady who can evict her tenant and still keep collecting rent.

What you pay

1154 Support is what you pay for love. Alimony is what you pay for hate.

Buy happiness

1155 Who says money can't buy happiness? I know at least six men who have bought divorces.

Fool's gold

1156 Fool's gold: alimony.

Bank on

1157 Alimony is something a woman can bank a lot on.

With or without

1158 Women! You can't live with them and you can't live without them — the alimony's too high.

Give their all

1159 Men should be willing to give their all for freedom, but usually the divorce court has to order them to.

APPEARANCE

Won't go away

1160 I neglect my appearance, yet I must say,
Though it's neglected it won't go away.

ASTRONAUTS

Auto accident

1161 Our moon astronauts have lots to worry about. They must be frightened to death that their wives and kids will get involved in a traffic accident while they're away.

AUTOMOBILES

Crawling with cars

1162 Our highways are crawling with cars. That's as fast as they can go.

On a dime

1163 I can stop my car on a dime — but I can't start it on one.

Competition

1164 We invented the nuclear bomb so we could give the auto some competition.

Get a car free

1165   I can tell you how to get a car free. The only charge will be theft.

Backed out of garage

1166   Then my wife backed out of the garage. That would have been fine if I hadn't just backed it in.

BABIES
Love my children

1167   I love my children, so I never had them.

Mistakes

1168   Mistakes are what send people to heaven, and bring them from there.

BACHELOR

Suppose that you're a bachelor who has just been told for the umpteenth nauseous time that eventually you'll fall in love and get married. These come-backs are sure to come in handy:

Loves with heart

1169   He who loves with his heart leads with his chin.

Soul mate

1170   I'm looking for a soul mate. I wouldn't want one in the flesh.

Days in court

1171   Love is valued most highly during the days of courting and the days in court.

Love bug

1172   The only shots that will protect me from the love bug seem to come from a gun.

Cupid

1173   Cupid is that mythical character who shoots arrows through the hearts of people to make them fall in love. More accurately, he shoots holes in their heads.

Bachelor in paradise

1174   "Bachelor in paradise" — that's like saying "a millionaire with money."

Women on crusade

1175 Women are on a crusade to make every single man miserable. They've already succeeded with the married ones.

Troubles

1176 Troubles never seem to come singly — only when you're married.

The question

1177   When asked the question, "What is bliss?"
A bachelor said, "A miss."
Two lovers said, "A kiss."
A married couple said, "This?"

BIKINI
Garb

1178 A bikini is a garb designed to keep women cool and men warm.

All the right places

1179 A girl with a bikini is one who's seen in all the right places.

BILLS
Keep up with Joneses

1180 I've managed to keep up with the Joneses — I've got just as many bills as they.

Withdrawal pains

1181 My wife is suffering withdrawal pains. There's nothing left in our account.

Interest

1182 Nowadays interest on a home is compounded at 8 percent and confounded at any percent.

CAPITAL PUNISHMENT
Premeditated

1183 Capital punishment is the worst because most premeditated of murders.

Approve of capital punishment

1184 Many murderers are so irrational, bloody and cruel that they would approve of capital punishment. So why shouldn't we?

CENSORS
Horrible things
1185 Censors want to censor pornography because sex is capable of making people do such horrible things. And if you don't believe it, look what it makes censors do.

Ban-the-Book
1186 Few people approve of the Ban-the-Bomb movement, but many support Ban-the-Book action. This shows which is of the greatest concern to people.

Banning together
1187 The anti-obscenity people believe in banning together.

CLOTHES
Make a woman
1188 New clothes don't make a man, but they can surely make a woman.

Reversible wedding dresses
1189 I understand they sell reversible wedding dresses to be used for the second wedding.

Bikini
1190 Bikini: A fishing net used to trap men.

Suppose that you're a fellow standing on the street corner with another fellow, watching the girls go by. Nine chances out of ten you'll be criticizing their clothes with something like this:

Devil take hindermost
1191 Every time I look at girls in trousers I think, "May the devil take the hindermost."

Slacks
1192 Slacks on women usually make the most of a bad thing.

Unadorned
1193 Hell hath no fury like a woman unadorned.

Great imagination
1194 The designer who dreamed up miniskirts had a great imagination, but he killed any need for ours.

Birthday suits

1195 Women's dresses look awful, their headgear's old hat;
Their skirts are immodest, their slacks worse than that.
When men take a look, that garb sure can scare 'em!
Yet as bad as their clothes are, it's good women wear them,
For the only raiment that could draw more hoots
Would be the same women in their birthday suits.

New miniskirts

1196 New miniskirts really know how to entice;
They seem to go up as fast as their price.

Keep it secret

1197 I can understand women's wearing the clothes they do nowadays. If I were a woman, I'd try to keep it a secret, too.

COMPLAINERS

Knocking opens doors

1198 Don't knock knocking. It opens many doors.

Close down the world

1199 I've had it! I'm going to close down the world.

Educated nerves

1200 I have educated nerves — they've been taut a lot.

Out of it

1201 I'd give the world to be out of it.

Bad as they seem

1202 Things are never as bad as they seem. Horrifying thought! — that means they can get worse.

COURTSHIP

Merry-go-round

1203 Courtship is a merry-go-round in which those who get the gold ring win, all others lose.

Just one damned thing

1204 Courtship is just one damned thing after another.

Moonlight blinds

1205 It's weird, but as bright as sunlight is, it doesn't blind as many people as moonlight does.

Glimpse of paradise

1206 An engagement is a glimpse of paradise on the way to hell.

CYNICS

Rather be

1207 We cynics would rather be hardhearted than softheaded.

Skeptic ulcers

1208 A pessimist ultimately gets skeptic ulcers.

See what he likes

1209 Every man sees in life what he likes. That includes cynics.

Definition

1210 Cynic: One who is enough to make anyone a pessimist.

Task of cynic

1211 The task of the cynic is the same as that of a housewrecker: he destroys so that something better can be built.

Double negative

1212 A cynic likes to use a double negative.

Suppose that someone has accused you, disparagingly, of being a cynic. You try to enlighten him about your lofty function:

Job of the cynic

1213 The job of the cynic is not to tell you what is true, but rather what is not.

Rare men

1214 A cynic is one of those rare men who doesn't predict calamity for the world. He believes it's already here.

Not optimistic

1215 I'd like to believe the world is going to be destroyed, but I'm not that optimistic.

Loathsome type

1216 A cynic is a loathsome type of person who makes you appear guilty of something you did do.

DATING (AND RELATED ACTIVITIES)

One long struggle

1217 Life's just one long struggle for a girl who's plain,
And a much longer struggle for a good-looking Jane.

Deadline

1218 Remember your deadline — the one that doesn't get the girl.

Glands

1219 Beauty is in the glands of the beholder.

Ugly sister

1220 I prayed to my fairy godmother to get me a date. Alas, she had this ugly sister...

Best defense

1221 When it comes to women, the best defense is offensiveness.

Take lots of care

1222 Take lots of care when you choose your wife;
You want the right one to ruin your life.

Freedom of Press

1223 When he asked if she believed in freedom of the press,
Without hesitation she resounded "Yes!"
But when he exercised freedom by giving her a squeeze,
She forgot what she'd said and gave him the breeze.

Hims

1224 The only thing she likes about church are the hims.

No man's land

1225 She had a nightmare that she was lost in no-man's land.

Laying on of hands

1226 "I slapped my boy friend when he said 'Bless you'."
"For saying 'Bless you'?"
"No, for the accompanying laying on of hands."

Well-meaning friends

1227 I have well-meaning friends who are always getting me blind dates. They sure give me the creeps.

Sweep off feet

1228 A man who sweeps a girl off her feet may soon find her landing right on top of him.

Wrong aim

1229 Girl to Masher: "Listen, buster, I don't know what your goal is, but your aim is all wrong."

Fresh-stale

1230   To a girl, a man who isn't fresh is stale.

Definitions

1231   *Mandate:* The type all girls pray for.
Perfumes: Scents to make a man lose his.
Kissing: Just two saps, touching yaps.
Dating: A system under which a man pays for the privilege of giving a girl an evening of entertainment, compliments, putting coats on, wit, conversation, etc. Sometimes the more brutish men insist on a kiss for payment; if the girl enjoys kissing also, she gives it to him.
Stuffed date: One you've taken to the most expensive restaurant in town.

Suppose that your newly pubescent son has just asked you for your opinions on dating (believe it or not!). Display your wisdom with one of these:

Not much substance

1232   A girl who can be picked up doesn't have much substance.

Contempt of courting

1233   I plead guilty to contempt of courting.

Pleasure and business

1234   Dating is a case of mixing pleasure with business. The man seeks pleasure and the girl means business.

Girl's clutches

1235   Son, remember that necking can put you in a girl's clutches.

DIVORCE

Not hard enough

1236   We have so much divorce because it isn't hard enough for people to get married. It should be made impossible.

Admit faults

1237   Divorcees will admit they had faults which helped cause their divorces, but not any more — they divorced them.

Gives her everything

1238   When a man gives his name to a woman, he gives her everything. The law sees to that.

Unbearable

1239 No matter how unbearable a husband finds his wife, he's still forced to support her.

Invitation

1240 You are cordially invited to the divorce proceedings of and_____, to be held in_____Courtroom on_____. Entertainment provided.

Everything I own

1241 Everything I own or ever will own I owe to my wife. That's what the judge said when he gave her a divorce.

Takes two

1242 It takes two to cause a divorce: the wife and her lawyer.

Many faults

1243 I do have many faults, but I'm divorcing them.

Divorce definitions

1244 The putting away of childish things.

A legal proceeding at which it is decided how much allowance the husband will be given from his income.

A financial transaction in which a man parts with his assets to get rid of his major liability.

A parting of the ways and means.

Heart failure.

When a man surrenders all he owns, or ever will, to relieve his wife of all responsibility.

Sex appeal

1245 Sex appeal: The appeal that always wins in a divorce case.

Child support

1246 Child support: maternal revenue.

Ransom

1247 What a man spends on his date is charity, what he spends on his wife is tribute, and what he spends on his ex-wife is ransom.

Battle fatigue

1248 Most divorces are caused by battle fatigue.

A terrible thing

1249 Divorce is a terrible thing which should always be avoided —
by not getting married.

Funeral expenses

1250 At the death of a marriage, the man has to pay the funeral
expenses.

Tenth anniversary

1251 I'm celebrating my tenth anniversary. I've been divorced ten
years.

*Suppose that someone you know (a man) has just been di-
vorced. Naturally you'll talk about his situation whenever you
get a chance. Maybe some of the following comments will
come in handy:*

Sea of troubles

1252 He was drowning in a sea of troubles when his wife came to
his rescue — by divorcing him.

His fault

1253 Really, his divorce was his own fault. He made a horrible mistake — by getting married.

Took a pill

1254 When he got depressed he took a pill, but she soon divorced
him.

First anniversary

1255 He celebrated his first wedding anniversary with a divorce.

Only way out

1256 For any husband, the only way out of a marriage is through
the wringer.

DOCTORS

Daily billing

1257 Doctors are going to start sending out bills daily so they'll
reach the patient while the body is still warm.

Stick out tongue

1258 Doctors are people you stick your tongue out to.

DOGS
Friendly
1259 Dogs don't know as much as humans. That's why they're so friendly.

EARTHQUAKE
Generous to a fault
1260 The Californians go on building just as though there'll never be another earthquake. They're generous to a fault.

EATING
Grub
1261 "Eat your grub," mother yelled, "before it crawls away!"

Caviar
1262 Caviar is a food sold to the wealthy by Russia, a country which believes in making the rich suffer and knows how to do it

Cake, too
1263 Americans believe the Bible when it says man cannot live by bread alone. They insist on cake, too.

Epitaph
1264 Epitaph: Health foods and fads he found mighty dear.
They surely were that; they put him here.

EPITAPHS
Hope he squirms
1265   Here lies my husband;
    I hope he squirms
    When he's eaten by some
    Of those other worms.

Suspicion
1266   I hope I fare well,
    But I've just a suspicion:
    Death won't pay me
    As it did my mortician.

Four leaf clover
1267   No flowers for me
    When you cover me over.

Just give me your hopes
And a four leaf clover.

Paradise

1268   In paradise, alone,
His soul will dwell;
When he arrives there,
Others will go to hell.

Fugitive from bathtub

1269   Such a fugitive from the bathtub
Was this young pup,
There was no need at his burial
To cover him up.

Pest

1270   Inside this grave there lies a pest.
He and the living are now at rest.

His goal

1271   Getting gorgeous girls
Was his goal.
One of them put him
In this hole.

Out of the hole

1272   He spent his life getting out of the hole so he could end in
this one.

Permanently planted

1273   He was permanently planted while alive.

Rather be

1274   I'd rather be alive
Wrong
Than dead
Right.

EXCUSES

Never make a fool

1275   I can never make a fool of someone who doesn't help me.

Sincere clod

1276   The next time I'm repulsive, remember that it's better to have
a sincere clod than an insincere gentleman.

Love enemies

1277 Sure I have a lot of foes. But then, I love my enemies and like to love as many people as possible.

Going to bed

1278 I don't like going to bed. I'd rather it came to me.

Lot of resting

1279 You can't say I never do anything — I do a lot of resting.

Christian

1280 Of course I'm a Christian. But it's the character of other Christians that makes me keep it a secret.

Bad jokes

1281 I admit the jokes I tell you are pretty bad. I wouldn't waste a good one on you.

Not married

1282 I'm not married yet because I haven't convinced any girl that I'm sufficiently worthless to deserve her.

Suppose that you're constantly being accused of laziness, in which case you try to justify yourself or at least explain your inactions. Some of these excuses may help you out of a dilemma without straining your mental muscles:

No such thing

1283 There's no such thing as *good* hard work.

Layaway plan

1284 My layaway plan is to sleep for 24 hours every day.

Man of principle

1285 I'm a man of principle, but I won't stand up for my cause.

Lying down

1286 It makes my wife mad that I take her nagging lying down.

Lot out of work

1287 I get a lot out of work — sweat, fatigue, myself.

Hard worker

1288 I'm really a hard worker by instinct — but I always fight my baser instincts.

What's your excuse?

1289   I didn't do that job because I'm lazy. What's your excuse?

Labor pains

1290   Around work I'm like a pregnant woman — I have acute labor pains.

Life's work

1291   I've made it my life's work to avoid work.

FINANCE

It's not true

1292   It's not true that taxes take most of a man's income. Alimony does.

Family fortune

1293   I inherited the family fortune — me.

Just barely

1294   How do I manage with money? Just barely.

More blessed

1295   It's more blessed to give than to receive. The Internal Revenue Service has seen to that.

All I know

1296   For all I know, I should be paid millions.

Not enough talents

1297   I don't get rich because I don't have enough talents. Though I'm a superb writer, craftsman, inventor, etc., I don't know how to cheat.

FLORIDA

Waving palms

1298   Florida is a land of waving palms, waiting for a tip.

FRIEND

Best friend

1299   "My wife ran away with my best friend."
       "How long had you known him?"
       "Oh, I never met him."

FUNERALS
Death toll
1300 Anyone who doesn't think the death toll is high should have to pay for a funeral.

Suppose that you've just listened to a funeral eulogy about someone you disliked. You can't help thinking, or even commenting, in the following vein:

All men perfect
1301 Death makes all men perfect. If you don't believe it, just listen to a funeral eulogy.

Lived frugally
1302 He lived frugally all his life so he could spend more than he could afford to die.

Warm feeling
1303 When I think of where he's going, I get a warm feeling all over.

Generous
1304 Believing a funeral eulogy is the only time we can afford to be generous with someone.

GAMBLING
Chronic gambler
1305 Chronic gambler: One who doesn't miss a bet.

GIRLS
Good enough
1306 I guess girls are good enough — and I believe in letting good enough alone.

Shallowness
1307 It's shallowness for a man to marry a girl just because she's good looking. She should have money, too.

Nightmare
1308 To girl: "Have you ever had a nightmare in which a man was chasing you and you couldn't stop running?"

Sugar'n spice
1309   Sugar'n spice and all that's nice,
      Until she grows up and leads to rice.

GOSSIP
Can never tell
1310 You can never tell about people, unless you're a gossip.

GOVERNMENT
Ship of fools
1311 The ship of state is a ship of fools.

Injustices
1312 We just can't tolerate all these mob-caused injustices! They must be confined to the courts and legislatures.

Paperweight
1313 Bureaucrat: Paperweight.

Pay dirt
1314 Grassroots government is closer to the pay dirt.

HEALTH
Headache
1315 I've got a headache all over my body.

Bad climate
1316 No wonder those people are unhealthy. With their climate, their lungs are always full of water.

Credo
1317 Hypochondriac's credo: Where there's a will there's an ill.

HENPECKING
Master
1318 Have you noticed? They address a human male as master only when he's a child.

Loved and lost
1319 It's better to have loved and lost
Than to have loved and then been bossed.

Control
1320 A woman can easily control a man with one finger — if it has his wedding ring on it.

Suppose that one of your gang is finally taking the fatal step, and you're all commiserating with him, trying to make him feel worse than he already does. It's likely that some sadist will come up with one or more of the following

Under her feet

1321   The only time a wife wants her husband under her feet is when she's walking on him.

Lesser of two evils

1322   A woman usually marries a man who is the lesser of two evils. She's the first.

Made to order

1323   Most wives think they're made to order.

Number 10

1324   Marriage is signified by the number 10. She's the one and he's the zero.

Lord and master

1325   When a wife says her husband is lord and master, that's just a compliment of the management.

Become one

1326   They say that when a man and a woman get married they become one, but that's only because he becomes nothing.

Stay on toes

1327   When you get married you'll have to stay on your toes or you'll wind up on your knees.

Suppose that the married guys in your gang are sympathizing with each other (don't they always?). It would be hard to top their tales of woe, but maybe one or more of these will be useful in a pinch:

Out of order

1328   My wife is always out of order, but never out of orders.

Decision-making

1329   I get to help in the decision-making process in our house. My wife doesn't know what we're not going to do until she finds out what I want to do.

Agrees

1330   Marriage agrees with me, but my wife doesn't.

All the talking

1331   It's not true a wife wants to do all of the talking. She does want her husband to say "yes."

Commanding personality

1332   My wife has a commanding personality. And believe me, I obey!

Understanding

1333   My wife and I have an understanding: she is never to ask me to do housework, and I'm to just do it.

HUSBANDS

Behave

1334   How do most husbands behave when they're away from their wives? They don't.

Co-despondent

1335   He named another husband as a co-despondent.

Works hard

1336   An American husband is a man who works hard at two jobs so he can buy labor-saving appliances to make his housework easier.

No self-control

1337   Husband: a man with no self-control.

INDIANS

Without reservations

1338   The Indians want their freedom without any reservations.

JOBS

Time clock sign

1339   Time clock sign: "We will now observe eight hours of silence, out of respect for our jobs."

Hit the clock

1340   "I'm going to go hit the time clock."
"Is it time to leave?"
"No, that's why I'm going to hit it."

Fire-power

1341   He's the boss. He has the fire-power.

Unemployment insurance

1342   The best unemployment insurance policy is loafing.

Automaton

1343   If you want to keep your job in this age of automation, become
an automaton.

*Suppose that you're a boss — and if you're a boss, then
you're certain to find it necessary to stimulate some of your
employees now and then with not-so-subtle comments and
memos. Some of these may help in your employee-relations
program:*

Do anything you wish

1344   This company is liberal. You are allowed to do anything you
wish except complain about what you aren't allowed to do.

Vegetable

1345   In this field, consider yourself a vegetable who'll get canned
the moment you get fresh.

Isn't stubborn

1346   The boss doesn't want to fire you, but he isn't stubborn.

Ready to help

1347   If you think you'd be ahead someplace else, we're ready to
help you advance yourself.

Coffee breaks

1348   Your coffee breaks are to relieve your work, not replace it.

Lucky

1349   The boss is lucky to have you here, but don't crowd his luck.

Quitting bell

1350   The quitting bell in this office was not installed to be an alarm
clock.

No more sneezing

1351   There's to be no more sneezing on the job. It spreads germs
and wastes time.

Often fired

1352   Those hired are often fired.
Those fired are seldom hired.

A dream

1353   You'll find this job a dream if you don't.

JUDGES

Only human

1354   When judges make mistakes we should realize they are only human. It's too bad they don't agree.

Justice in court

1355   One case of justice being done in a court of law was when the judge had a heart attack and died on the spot.

Contempt of court

1356   Judges should be arrested for encouraging contempt of court.

Court of Honor

1357   A Court of Honor is one where they don't have judges.

Make mistakes

1358   Justice is not entirely unknown to courts of law. Judges have been ĸnown to make mistakes.

KIDS

Drawing rooms

1359   I have six drawing rooms in my house — the kids have drawn on all the walls in the place.

Tolerant

1360   My kids are very tolerant. When I tell them to do something they don't mind at all.

Dangerous animals

1361   Children are potentially dangerous animals. They become adults.

New generation

1362   They say all of us have to die sometime in order to make room for the new generation. But considering the quality of the new generation, I'm not going to cooperate.

Mistake

1363   Most kids are the result of a mistake — marriage.

Not very bright

1364 Father to son: "Son, I can't deny I'm not very bright. You're the living proof of it."

Paddle

1365 Paddle: A piece of wood used to propel and guide both boats and children.

Leaps and bounds

1366 My family is growing by leaps and bounds — all leaps and no bounds.

Punishes

1367 The father punishes the children, the mother punishes the father, and the kids punish both mother and father.

Just society

1368 In a just society, parents would have to get their children's consent before bringing them into the world.

Know so little

1369 Childhood is when we know so little we think our parents know everything. Adulthood is when we know so little we think we know everything.

Babe in arms

1370 If you want a babe in arms, you've got to take a babe in arms.

Adolescence

1371 Adolescence: Ignorance not yet fully matured.

Generation gap

1372 Generation gap: A phenomenon occasioned by the fact that young people see their parents as proof the world should be improved, while the parents see their kids as proof it can't or won't be.

LAW

Ignorance

1373 The ignorance of the law is no excuse.

Lawsuit

1374 Lawsuit: The type that takes you to the cleaners.

LAWYERS
Claim jumpers
1375   Lawyers are a bunch of claim jumpers.

Innocent by contrast
1376   A lawyer is a man who makes his dishonest clients look innocent — by contrast.

LAZY RELATIVES
Can't smile
1377   My brother-in-law can't work up a smile because he can't smile at anything that involves work.

All of his time
1378   My uncle spends all of his time resting so he won't be too tired to do anything important that might come along.

Insomnia
1379   My uncle is troubled with insomnia — so afraid he'll get it that he can't sleep more than twelve hours a day.

Ill at ease
1380   My brother-in-law is never ill at ease; in fact, he's always happy at ease.

Gets so tired
1381   When my uncle thinks of all the work his body does just to stay alive — heart pumping, stomach churning, lungs working, etc. — he gets so tired he has to lie down.

LIARS
Not happy
1382   *Sam:* "When you call me a liar, smile!"
Jim: "Why? I'm not happy you're one."

LIFE
Bed of roses
1383   The damn fool who said life is a bed of roses never tried to get through one.

Can't live without it
1384   I don't like life, but I've found I can't live without it.

Worth leaving

1385 Life's not even worth leaving.

Death insurance

1386 Life insurance is a waste of money because it's actually death insurance — and who needs insurance for that eventuality?

LOVE

Slot machine

1387 I put a nickel in the slot machine of love and hit a lemon.

Culmination-termination

1388 Sex is the culmination of love; marriage its termination.

Disappointed in love

1389 Have you heard of the fellow who was disappointed in love three times? One girl refused to marry him, and the other two accepted.

Suppose that you've been musing about love and its meaning (who hasn't?). Of course you've come to some profound conclusions, maybe some of them like these:

Foundation

1390 A man who is so much in love he's walking on air doesn't have much of a foundation for marriage.

Hard to sleep

1391 A man in love finds it hard to get any sleep until he wakes up.

Love his enemy

1392 The existence of romance proves that man can love his enemy.

Faithful

1393 A man should always be faithful to his loved one — he shouldn't care what his wife thinks.

Bound to be bound

1394 A man in love is bound to be bound.

No longer in love

1395 You can tell a woman's no longer in love when she comes down out of the clouds and plants her feet firmly on her husband.

MARIJUANA

Go to pot

1396 Marijuana smokers want the world to go to pot.

Busy

1397 He's always busy at the plant.

MARRIAGE

Marriage counseling

1398 Marriage counseling usually comes too late. The marriage has already taken place.

Common goal

1399 To have a happy marriage, a couple should work together toward a common goal — divorce.

Burden of pleasing

1400 When men and women find the burden of trying to please each other too onerous, they either break off their relationship or get married.

Leash on life

1401 Marriage can give a woman a new leash on life.

Advice to girls

1402 Advice to girls: To get a ring on your finger, wrap a man around it first.

Married before

1403 *Minister:* "Do you, John Marshall, take this woman to be your wedded wife?"
Bride: "Oh, John Marshall is your name? Say, haven't I been married to you before?"

Commitment paper

1404 Marriage license: Commitment paper.

Warfare

1405 Marriage is the only form of warfare in which the armies clash only after their engagement is over.

Proof of ownership

1406 Marriage certificate: The wife's proof of ownership.

Discounted bonds

1407 The bonds of matrimony are being discounted.

Out of clinches

1408 In marriage, as in boxing, the real fight starts when you come out of the clinches.

Marriage is collision

1409 Marriage is the collision that comes from getting too close to each other as we travel life's highway.

Marriage vow

1410 Marriage vow: "Never again!"

Divine institution

1411 Marriage is a divine institution. It's certainly not for people.

Strictly for women

1412 Marriage is strictly for women — and believe me, they are strict!

Losing proposition

1413 When a man's proposal of marriage is accepted, it's a losing proposition.

Confucius says

1414 Confucius says: "Man who gets married is unfaithful — to self."

Grateful

1415 I'm grateful for every single day. But it's my married days that make me appreciate them.

Wonderful institution

1416 Marriage is a wonderful institution that should never be demeaned or sullied by entering it.

Blood tests

1417 They shouldn't give blood tests to those who want to get married. They should give brain tests.

Hopes to get

1418 The only thing a rational man hopes to get out of marriage is himself.

Sweden

1419 "They have trial marriages in Sweden."
"I thought all marriages were trials."

Devoted

1420 My girl has devoted her life to making me happy. She married someone else.

Sentence

1421 In a marriage, the minister pronounces the sentence and the wife carries it out.

Sea of matrimony

1422 The sea of matrimony is not the Pacific.

Right to marry

1423 Every man has a right to get married — and that's the last right he has.

Golden wedding

1424 They call them golden wedding anniversaries because they're so rare.

Misplaced "I"

1425 A misplaced "I" in the marital state
Will sometimes make it a martial state.

Definitions

1426 Courtship and marriage classes: Classes that are low on the academic scale, taught to those low on the evolutionary scale.

Marriage: A game of love in which all of the players lose.

Bride: The bill of goods the groom has bought himself.

Marriage: A three-ring circus — engagement ring, wedding ring and suffering.

Marriage: The mathematics by which 1 & 1 makes 2, or 3, or 4, or ---.

Marriage: An institution in which the woman is a helpmate and the man is an inmate

Marriage: Paradise, lost. A church ceremony followed by a period of mourning.

MISCELLANEOUS

Age will tell

1427 Age will tell — but the one who owns it won't.

Sell to me

1428 "Will you sell that to me?"
"By all your means!"

Camping

1429 Anyone who has ever gone camping knows why it's called the forest prime evil.

Ireland

1430 "Why will Ireland soon be too large?"
"I don't know, why?"
"Because it keeps Dublin."

No fool

1431 There's no fool like an old fool who's managed to outlive the rest.

If I were young

1432 If I were young and knew what I know now, I wouldn't learn what I know now.

Wages of sin

1433 The wages of sin are doubly blessed: there's the fun of earning them, and they're not taxable.

Staying power

1434 Staying Power: What people have when you want to go to bed.

MONEY

Earn more money

1435 How to earn more money than you desire: Lower your desires.

Gold

1436 Gold: A precious metal so valuable as to be worth its weight in beef.

Easy go

1437 I've found money is not easy to acquire, but that's the way it goes.

Soft soap

1438 To clean up, use soft soap.

Sound money

1439 Sound money is that which talks the loudest.

Gold standard

1440 America has a gold standard. So does everyone I know.

Smell of success

1441 The smell of success is that of mint.

Cave or hole

1442 With houses costing what they do, we can choose between living in a cave or in the hole.

Worth its weight

1443 Gold: A metal worth its weight in beef.

Suicides

1444 Insurance companies won't pay on suicides. Otherwise everybody would be killing himself to get rich.

Old-timer

1445 An old-timer is a man who can remember when a dollar was worth fifty cents.

How-to-succeed

1446 How-to-succeed books are those which teach you how to make a lot of money — by writing how-to-succeed books.

Coinage motto

1447 The motto on American coinage is, "In this God we trust."

In my house

1448 In my house what I save goes.

MOVIES

True story

1449 "This movie is a true story. Only the names, dialogue, and actions have been changed in order to protect the producer against loss and the viewers against gain."

NOT-SO-NUTTY NOTIONS
Have government pay
1450 Have the government pay all legal expenses for persons accused of crimes but acquitted.

Divorce refuge
1451 Have Nevada or some other foreign country become a refuge for divorced men. This would likely become a lucrative industry, such as gambling.

Christmas shopping
1452 When Christmas shopping this year, pick out next year's presents, lay them away, and have a whole year to pay.

Free funerals
1453 Since free vacations are awarded to anyone recruiting ten others to go along, why not arrange the same plan for funerals?

Suicide kit
1454 Sell a suicide kit containing a fatal poison for the act, liquor to bring courage, and a rationale as an excuse.

Tilting chair
1455 Design a chair that will automatically tilt at intervals, changing position for a lazy occupant.

Tax tobacco
1456 Why not tax tobacco products and use the proceeds for anti-smoking ads?

NUDITY
Nudist colony
1457 Nudist colony: Where people are all together in the altogether.

OVERWEIGHT
Suppose that everybody has an opinion on how to lose weight, or the futility of trying. Can you top these?

Exercise
1458 If exercise would really make a person lose weight, carrying fifty extra pounds around should do it.

Ten deep breaths

1459   To reduce, take ten deep breaths every day — nothing else.

Reducing machines

1460   Somebody should develop food vending machines especially
for dieters. When they put money in, nothing comes out.

Fat girls, remember

1461   Fat girls, remember: It's only when there's less of you that
men want to see more of you.

Reducing salon

1462   Reducing salon: A place that takes its pound of flesh.

PAINTING

Artists

1463   Painters have to be artists to make people think they're painters.

PARKING

Hot rod

1464   He's got a hot rod that makes him smile —
Takes but half a minute to cover a mile.
The rod's even better when it comes to sparking;
He makes better time while the car is parking.

PHILOSOPHY

Boring time

1465   Youth is the boring time when your future lies ahead of you.
Old age is the boring time when your future is behind you.

Nagging

1466   The only thing nagging convinces a man of is that he hates
nagging.

Dirty joke

1467   A dirty joke is one that's pulled on you.

Conscience

1468   One should respect his conscience only if it deserves respect.

Tolerance

1469   We should all be tolerant — so please be tolerant of my in-
tolerance!

Agitator

1470 It takes an agitator to get out the dirt.

Under pressure

1471 People, like air, get hot under pressure.

Civil rights

1472 Why such a fight for civil rights? I thought everyone had the right to be civil.

Good old days

1473 The only good thing there ever was about the good old days is memories.

No sin

1474 If there were no religions, moralists, or laws, there would be no sin.

Too many oughts

1475 There are too many "oughts" in this world, and all oughts add up to zero.

Self-righteousness

1476 Self-righteousness gives one the advantage of righteousness without its necessity.

RACE PREJUDICE

Color line

1477 The color line is a pigment of the imagination.

Hate

1478 I'm race prejudiced — I hate the human race.

I believe

1479 I believe in treating all races the same — with the utmost contempt.

Whites

1480 Whites: People whose fairness is only skin deep.

White lie

1481 The concept of colored inferiority is just a white lie.

RAPE

Volunteer

1482 Protect yourself against rape. Volunteer!

REJECTIONS

Suppose that you have been asked to go out by someone whom you neither wish to date nor hurt. Here are some diplomatic dillies that may come to your rescue:

Stupid

1483 Anybody would have to be stupid not to want a date with you, and I'm sure you don't want to date somebody that's stupid.

Computer cards

1484 We may get along famously, but our computer cards are incompatible.

Better taste

1485 You're too good for me — your taste is better than mine.

Republican

1486 You have to be democratic to want to date me, and I'm a Republican.

Dream man

1487 You're such a dream man, I don't want to risk dating you and then waking up.

As you are

1488 I'd rather remember you as you are; I don't want to find out your faults.

Reasonable

1489 I can't give reasons — I'm not a reasonable girl.

Inferior

1490 You make me feel inferior.

Doesn't appreciate

1491 I can't let you spend money on someone who doesn't appreciate you enough to let you spend money on her.

Marvelous gift

1492 I don't accept gifts from a man I'm not married to, and a date with you is a marvelous gift.

Sacrifice

1493 I'd sacrifice anything to go out with you, except myself.

Suppose that you have been asked to go out by someone you

don't like, and you don't care if that someone knows it. In that case you probably know just what to say, but in the event you suffer a momentary loss of recall, just toss off one of these:

No

1494 I guess I'm going to have to think of a wittier way of saying it — NO!

Strange men

1495 I don't go out with strange men, and you're one of the strangest men I know.

Passionate

1496 I can't trust myself around you. I get too passionate — I want to hit you.

Last date

1497 You remember our last date? Well, that's what it was!

Can't go

1498 I can't go out with you. I'm busy — thinking up reasons why I can't go out with you.

SEX

Great problem

1499 Sex is a great problem to me. In fact, I find everything about it great.

Worst thing

1500 The worst thing about sex is the sex you've got to associate with to get it.

Flip a coin

1501 All men figuratively flip a coin to decide whether to get married. If heads win, they don't; if tails win, they do.

Evil

1502 Sex is evil — it makes men want to get married.

Stupid

1503 One time in my life I really felt stupid, and boy, did she slap my face!

Loose

1504 Nothing makes a person become loose faster than becoming tight.

Ideal combination

1505 Ideal combination: A girl with an hourglass figure who doesn't know the time of day.

Yet to be made

1506 A beautiful woman who has yet to be made has yet to be made.

Fun?

1507 Is it fun? Heaven forbids!

Nymphomaniac

1508 Give her some men who are stouthearted men and she'll ask for ten thousand more.

Wine and women

1509   I'll readily confess I don't care about song,
                   But I like a life of wine, women and wrong.

Falsies

1510 *Falsies:* Breastworks.

Way of all flesh

1511 He's never gone the way of all flesh — only the good looking flesh.

Wanton women

1512 Wanton women want not.

Appeal

1513 What makes women especially appealing is that the rest of us are men.

Melody

1514 A pretty girl is like a melody — it takes a lot of notes to make one.

SILLY SYLLOGISMS
Lung cancer

1515 Cigarettes cause lung cancer. People are willing to spend a fortune on cigarettes but wish they didn't cost so much. *Moral:* There's a fortune waiting for the man who can give people lung cancer for less money.

Crime

1516 Big business brings efficiency and a higher standard of living for all. Crime is big business. *Moral:* Crime is good.

Fools

1517 Premise 1: The fewer fools in the world, the better off we are. Premise 2: People who smoke are fools because smoking is a killer. Conclusion: People should smoke because it gets rid of fools.

Self-righteousness

1518 Self-righteousness is bad. Moral: Righteousness is good only for others.

Don't marry family

1519 One should not marry members of one's family. All humans belong to the same family. Moral: Don't get married.

SMOKING

Weed

1520 Cigarettes are known as weeds because they sprout from uncultivated areas.

Walk a mile

1521 He'd walk a mile for a cigarette, but since he's a smoker he can't walk that far.

Snuff

1522 He who smokes cigarettes is not up to snuff.

Stamp out

1523 Anti-smoking slogan: Stamp out cigarettes and smokers!

New holder

1524 They have a new holder that makes cigarettes safe. It's called a garbage can.

TAXES

Free country

1525 This may be a free country, but its government certainly is expensive!

Pound of flesh

1526   The bite which the government takes from every taxpayer is a pound of flesh.

Oil rig

1527   Oil rig: The depletion allowance.

Bachelor taxes

1528   Bachelor taxes: The bind that ties.

Conservatives

1529   Conservatives are not entirely selfish. They are willing to spend taxes on killing.

Uncle Sam

1530   It must be that white beard of Uncle Sam's that makes everybody think he is Santa Claus.

Property tax

1531   Property tax is making it very difficult for a man to hold his ground.

TEARS

Tears

1532   Tears: Headwaters.

TELEPHONE

Crank call

1533   Remember when a crank call was made with a crank telephone?

TELEVISION

Bad habit

1534   Television is one bad habit that can be easily broken.

New American

1535   When anyone calls to see the New American, he checks the TV schedule to see when he's free.

Light without illumination

1536   Television: A box that throws off light without illumination.

Wasteland

1537   How can TV be a wasteland when it's so full of fertilizer?

Fresh air

1538   Eventually they hope to transmit smell over television through the nose as well as the eyes and ears. When this happens the younger generation might learn what fresh air smells like.

Vacuum tube

1539 What TV gives you is just what you'd expect to get from a vacuum tube.

No vision

1540 Television is all sight and sound and no vision.

Television set

1541 Television set: That one on the viewers' faces.

Movie houses

1542 Movie houses are showing commercials now to compete with television by making their patrons feel at home.

Ignorance

1543 Television spends billions to increase the total amount of ignorance in the world.

Its best

1544 Commercial television does its best to do its worst.

TRUTH

Truth will tell

1545 The truth will tell, but it would be rewarded more if it kept its mouth shut.

Lose a friend

1546 To tell the truth. . . that's the way to lose a friend.

UNISEX STYLES

Test of sex

1547 They've been trying to perfect a test for years that will tell the sex of human beings before they're born. Now a test should be devised to tell their sex after they're grown up.

Boys and men

1548 It used to be boys who had to prove they were men. Now it's the women, too.

One from another

1549 A boy is a boy and a girl is a girl;
Telling one from another makes the mind whirl.

Good old days

1550 I yearn for the good old days when a man was a man, and a woman wasn't.

How do you tell?

1551 It's easy to tell the men from the boys, but how do you tell the men from the women?

WAR

Still paying

1552 We didn't fight the last war for nothing. We're still paying for it.

Protest marches

1553 Protest marches: Marches that soldiers make, under protest.

WEDDINGS

Ornaments

1554 They're already renting all kinds of ornaments to the bride for weddings. Soon they'll begin renting the groom.

Receiving line

1555 The receiving line comes after the deceiving line.

Fashion craze

1556 The newest fashion craze is a combined wedding and maternity dress.

Worst odds

1557 Nevada gambling establishments offering the worst odds are the wedding chapels.

Veil

1558 Veil: What the bride wears over her eyes at the wedding, and what a groom wears over his eyes before the wedding.

WISDOM

Wise man

1559 A wise man is one who can take the offensive without being so.

True wisdom

1560 The true wisdom of the East resides in being able to make the West believe the East has some.

No such thing

1561 Wise is the man who knows there is no such thing as wisdom.

Certainly old

1562 The man who says age brings wisdom may not be wise, but he's certainly old.

WIVES

Favorite tune

1563 A wife's favorite tune is the one she can make her husband dance to.

Old and new

1564 Some wives seem to feel that before they can make a new man out of their husbands they must wreck the old.

Horseplay

1565 My wife's idea of horseplay is nagging me.

Broom

1566 Broom: What the wife rides when her husband says she can't drive the car.

Sidekicker

1567 Wife: A man's sidekicker.

Husband's goose

1568 All wives aren't good cooks, but most of them know how to cook their husband's goose.

Solomon

1569 The Bible is inconsistent, it seldom jives.
It says Solomon was wise, yet had many wives.

Folly

1570 There's naught that's folly in this long old life
That man won't embrace, including a wife.

No-how

1571 When it comes to being negative, my wife has the no-how.

WOMEN

Bear the women

1572 All women have to do is bear the children. The men have to bear the women.

Music

1573   Music is the silence of a woman's voice.

Fight

1574   Men fight over women for the chance to fight with them.

Don't like themselves

1575   Obviously, women don't like much about themselves. They
       dress like men and hide their sex, cut their hair short and dye
       what remains, pluck their eyebrows, and hide their face and
       lips beneath gobs of makeup.

All is fair

1576   All is fair in love and war. . . except the woman.

Strong wills

1577   Women have weak bodies but make up for it with strong wills.

WORK

Working conditions

1578   Improve working conditions — Remove the work!

Never embrace

1579   Like a plain, honest girl, work is to be extolled and appreciated
       but never embraced.

Something missing

1580   I can't help feeling that something is missing in our American
       way of life — a powered reclining chair, for example.

All in

1581   The man who goes all out is soon all in.

Labor-saving devices

1582   Americans work hard to buy labor-saving devices so they'll
       have more time to work hard to buy more labor-saving devices
       so they'll have more time. . . .

YOUTH

Too precious

1583   "Youth's too precious to waste on the young"
       Is a favorite song old men have sung.
             And to prove they mean just what they say,
       They marry women much younger than they.

Part IV
Ad Libs and Lines
for Special Occasions

Ad-men's meeting or
  convention
Award ceremonies
Baby showers
Bachelor parties
Bankers meeting
Barbers meeting
Birth control speech
Birthday parties
Bon voyage affair
Businessmen's
  conventions
Charity drives
Christmas parties
Church fund drives
Church sermons
Club meetings
Conservationist speech
Conservatives rally
Consumers rally
Cooking lessons
Courtship and marriage
  lecture
Debuts
Dedication ceremonies
Democratic convention
Dentists meetings
Doctors meetings

Ecologists meetings
Election campaign
  speech
Election victory speech
Employer's speech to
  employees
Engagement party (see
  Wedding or engage-
  ment showers)
Family reunions
Fathers and Sons outings
Father's Day speech
Funeral eulogies
Graduation exercises
Health lecture
Heckling (see "Insults
  and Putdowns")
Inspirational speeches
Introduction speech
Inventors conference
Lectures (general)
Liberals rally
Memorial Day speech
Moderator
Mothers and Daughters
  outing
Mother's Day speech
New Year's Eve party

Panel discussions
Pep talks
Personality
   improvement talk
Philosophy speech
Poetry readings
Police rally
Political rallies
Psychologists
   (discussions about)
P.T.A. meetings
Publishers convention
Radicals rally
Republican convention
Retirement ceremony or
   party
Revival meeting
Safety meeting or
   lecture
Sales meetings
School lectures
Scout meetings

Sports banquet
Stockholders meeting
Success talks
Sunday School lessons
Taxpayers meeting
Teachers convention
Temperance speech
Testimonial dinners
Thanksgiving dinners
Toastmaster
Toasts
Traffic experts convention
Training lecture
Travel agents
   convention
Travelogue
Union meeting
Wedding anniversaries
Wedding or engagement
   showers
Weddings
Women's lib speech

AD-MEN'S MEETING OR CONVENTION
Such crowds
1584 I've never seen such crowds of people who didn't go to see that movie.

Opportunity
1585 Be sure to learn the difference between letting opportunity knock and knocking opportunity.

Eskimos
1586 It's our job not only to sell refrigerators to Eskimos, but to get them to want an icemaker as well.

Manufacturers
1587 We, like our clients, are manufacturers. But ours is the more important function. They only make products. We manufacture desire. There is no value in anything that is not wanted.

AWARD CEREMONIES
Good for something
1588 These award ceremonies at least give our employees a chance to prove they're good for something — even if it's only an award.

Ulterior motive
1589 There's no ulterior motive in awarding you this watch, as there was with one fellow I know when he presented his boss with a watch. This fellow hoped the watch would be stolen, and while his boss was on the way to the police station to report the loss, the fellow hoped, his boss would slip on the ice and break a leg; then, while his boss was in the hospital, someone would break into his home and various other misfortunes would happen, and eventually, this fellow hoped, he'd get his boss's job.

Superb job
1590 When people told me you'd done a good job, I replied, "I wouldn't say that — I'd say it was a superb job!"

Extremely deserving
1591 A man you've never met thinks you're extremely deserving of this award because I've been telling him about you.

Kidded yourself

1592   I hope you haven't kidded yourself that you deserve this award
       — because you really do.

BABY SHOWERS

Bird refuge

1593   You've had so many storks visit your house, I fear they'll de-
       clare it a bird refuge.

Narrowing the gap

1594   There are almost four Chinese to every American. Please try
       to remember that narrowing that gap is too big a job for just
       one woman.

Affinity

1595   You seem to have such an affinity for storks, I believe you
       should join the Audubon Society.

New model

1596   What's the matter with your kids that you feel you must have
       a new model every year?

No Doz

1597   You're an admirable chemist as well as a new mother. You've
       just made your own No Doz.

Too late

1598   Card from expectant wife's husband:
       Your stomach grows and grows so great
       I can't get near you — alas, too late!

Replaced

1599   When you think how many people are replaced by pills, I'm
       glad your new baby wasn't.

BACHELOR PARTIES

Pillory

1600   They used to put a man in a pillory to make him look like a
       fool. Now they stand him in a receiving line.

Hang

1601   If a suitor doesn't watch it, he can hang at the end of his own
       line.

Hold your girl

1602 Hold your girl on your knee before marriage and over it after marriage.

Doomsday

1603 Doomsday — Groomsday.

Can't afford

1604 I can't afford to get married. I'm rich.

Disconsolate groom

1605 Disconsolate groom who lost the race,
Give the victor a gown of satin and lace.
Just remember that when you say "I do"
It's a gown to her but curtains for you.

Very soon say

1606 A groom is a man who'll very soon say
He wishes that he'd given the bride away.

BANKERS MEETING

Great interest

1607 Among us financiers, great interest is shown in great interest.

Credit

1608 A banker is a man who believes in giving credit where credit is not overdue.

Withdrawal symptoms

1609 We've found that when wives go without clothes, they develop withdrawal symptoms. The result is, we lose a number of bank accounts.

Far in debt

1610 Some people are so far in debt they're borrowing money to pay the interest on the money they owe.

Holding the bag

1611 As one deadbeat said, "I may not pay my debts, but I don't leave my creditors empty-handed — I leave them holding the bag."

Like a girdle

1612 Money-lender's motto: Money is like a girdle — the more you make it stretch, the more you have to show but the less you enjoy it.

BARBERS MEETING
Dirty hair

1613 Even the polite young men of today never get on their knees for a girl. They'd get their hair dirty.

Don't worry

1614 Don't worry about our boys' long hair. They'll cut it when they start tripping over it.

Give them an inch

1615 Boys and their hair! You give them an inch and they'll take it down to their feet.

Women's legs

1616 The longhairs have taken our business down so much we'll have to recoup by offering cut rates for shaving women's legs.

Abominable snowman

1617 They've finally discovered what the abominable snowman is — a hippie who'd heard that a planeload of grass crashed in the Himalayas.

BIRTH CONTROL SPEECH
Confinement before conception

1618 We've got so many pregnant ladies around that it's time their confinements came before conception.

Make a production

1619 The typical pregnant woman likes to make a production out of reproduction.

In labor

1620 Too many women and George Meany have been in labor most of their lives.

Birth to a nation

1621 To fecund woman: Are you trying to give birth to a nation?

Only a smear

1622 According to the smear test my wife was pregnant — but fortunately it was only a smear.

Accident

1623 The girl and her boyfriend had a car accident and she came through that untouched. But not before — that's what caused the accident.

BIRTHDAY PARTIES

Shangri-la

1624 If you're a day over twenty, you're living in Shangri-la.

Happy birthday

1625 You're not on speed, heroin, hashish, benzedrine, peyote, banana peels, glue, opium, marijuana, or LSD — but have a happy birthday anyway!

Rolls Royce

1626 I was going to buy you a Rolls Royce but didn't because friendship is worth more than material things, and I knew that if you owned such a car you wouldn't associate with the pauper I'd be if I bought it for you.

Nature forgot

1627 I didn't forget that you're a year older, but from the looks of you, nature did.

Million reasons

1628 I can think of a million reasons why I should congratulate you on your birthday. But even though you're not a millionaire, congratulations anyway!

Blowing candles

1629 It's your birthday. You should be blowing out a lot of candles instead of burning them.

National holiday

1630 Did you know your birthday falls on a national holiday? At least I think it should be.

Middle-aged people

1631 Birthdays are one of the few things that middle-aged people don't want and yet can't get enough of.

Like medicine

1632   At our age the only good thing to be said about birthdays is that they're like medicine — they're hard to take but we can't stay alive without them.

BON VOYAGE AFFAIR

Happy return

1633   May you have a pleasant journey and a happy return — with all those beautiful, falsified tax deductions on.

Light heart

1634   Have a happy vacation and enjoy the best. May you come back with your heart as light as your wallet!

Stomach's gain

1635   Bon voyage! Though we shall miss you, our loss means your stomach's gain.

A going-away present

1636   As a going-away present I'll tell you how to afford only the best and get a good long rest: Change your handwriting style and forge your own name on your credit cards, then claim they were stolen. Afterwards you can look forward to about ten years of rest.

BUSINESSMEN'S CONVENTIONS

Ledgerdemain

1637   A crooked accountant is one who practices ledgerdemain.

Busy signals

1638   You're all successful men, I know, because you're like a party line — always giving off busy signals.

Indecision

1639   Gentlemen, don't be like the indecisive boss who waits to hear what the rumors say he'll do, before he makes a decision.

Too many strikes

1640   Industry would have set a record production year, but it had too many strikes against it.

Point of no returns

1641   I'm afraid that some of us want to sell such superior products that we may pass the point of no returns.

Fellow investor

1642 I know a fellow investor who is still cleaning up on the stock market. He's now a janitor for the New York Stock Exchange.

Made a killing

1643 Many of us made a killing in the stock market. We killed all chances of getting our money back.

High prices

1644 Admittedly our prices are high, but that's so we'll never have to raise them.

Magnate

1645 He's a magnate who attracts people.

CHARITY DRIVES

Ring and wring

1646 Let this be your motto: Ring your prospect's doorbell, then wring his wallet.

Wring their hearts and then their wallets.

Begins at home

1647 If the people you call on tell you that charity begins at home, tell them that's why you're ringing their doorbells.

Like buying an auto

1648 Influence people to think of giving to charity as similar to buying an auto: they're just keeping ahead of the Joneses.

Clear conscience

1649 Look upon yourself as selling a clear conscience.

Collection agency

1650 Look upon yourself as being a collection agency.

Regret

1651 When some people give to charity they know they'll regret it till the day they die — but they'll be glad after that.

Warm words

1652 Make your words so warm they'll melt butter — and hearts.

Raising kids

1653 One fellow's attempt at raising money was like raising kids — it cost more than it brought in and only won ingratitude.

Moving tongue

1654   Remember when you talk that a tongue moved in just the right way can open a thousand purses.

Boring pitch

1655   Don't be so dull that when someone says, "I gave at the office," he really means, "I just had to listen to a boring pitch."

CHRISTMAS PARTIES

Strange coincidence

1656   Talk about strange coincidences! My kid found out the other day that Christ was born on Santa Claus Day.

Flood of happiness

1657   I hope the Yuletide brings you a flood of happiness.

Mr. X

1658   *Mr. X:* The man people know nothing about, such as the X in Xmas.

So much love

1659   Christmas is a day when our fellow men love us so much that they'll give us gifts such as ties, and we love them so much we'll wear their gifts.

Expensive and wild

1660   Some Christmas parties can get pretty expensive and wild. Afterwards the boss tries to keep the wolf away from his door while the secretary tries to keep the stork away.

CHURCH FUND DRIVES

Fireproofing

1661   Collection: A donation of a charitable nature which is paid to fireproof the donor.

Insurance

1662   *Epitaph:* His company prospered by insuring his life.
          Millions will be coming to his wife.
          For himself, he said with his dying breath,
          "Give a dollar to the church to insure my death."

Keep separate

1663   Most people like to keep business and pleasure separate. Principles and actions, too.

Roller coaster

1664 A roller coaster is an amusement park ride similar to church in that it induces people to pay their money in order to have the hell scared out of them.

Collection plate

1665 What churches need is a collection plate that sounds an alarm if a small donation is placed in it, and flashes lights for a large one.

Take it with you

1666 The only way you can take it with you is to give it away before you go.

CHURCH SERMONS

Holy Sabbath

1667 He keeps the Sabbath holy by not desecrating the church with his presence.

Principle-principal

1668 Many people consider principle to be like principal — it's to be kept only as long as it earns an income.

Price comes high

1669 He wouldn't sell *his* soul for a nickel. His price comes high. Not because he's honest, but because he has an inflated view of his soul.

God's children

1670 We're all God's children, and I'll bet that's just what he thinks.

Life after death

1671 A smart man always maintains that there's a life after death. If he's wrong he'll never know it, and if he's right he can gloat.

Approve of church

1672 Many people approve of seeing others in church because then they aren't trying to get *them* to go.

Wheel of fortune

1673 Conscience is the only wheel of fortune which always stops on the number paying the most money.

Gold

1674 Gold is similar to God in spelling and in the amount of reverence it receives.

God

1675   The god most people believe in couldn't get into heaven.

CLUB MEETINGS

Volunteers

1676   I'm about to ask for volunteers. All those in favor say "I."

Minutes

1677   Let's keep our business short lest the reading of the minutes turn into hours.

Let's keep our business short lest the Minutes turn into hours.

Easy chairs

1678   We need your help. This is not a rich man's club, so let's not sit back in our easy chairs.

Pay your dues

1679   Will you *please* pay your dues? If this is a club it certainly hasn't succeeded in hitting some of you right.

CONSERVATIONIST SPEECH

Preserve nature

1680   We've been accused of wishing to preserve nature for humanity by making certain that no human ever sees it.

Wild outdoors

1681   The only wild outdoors many of our children ever see now is lovers' lane.

Commune with nature

1682   Commune with nature! See it in its primitive state: get out of your cars and see what's on the other side of the billboards!

Leavable

1683   Urban America is a highly leavable place.

Energy

1684   Too many people conserve only human energy.

Fools

1685   Anti-conservationist argument: The fools who oppose the Miami airport don't realize that it will cut down on all those deaths caused by alligators.

Insane

1686 Let's face it: with conditions what they are today, a man has to be insane not to go out of his mind.

CONSERVATIVES RALLY

White corpuscles

1687 We are the white corpuscles of our nation's bloodstream!

Relief checks

1688 Horrors! A drive is underway to make it possible for people to pick up their relief checks from their cars.

Craven images

1689 Our college kids are pacifists. They worship craven images.

Full stomach

1690 One needs a full stomach to contemplate the miseries of the poor.

CONSUMERS RALLY

TV

1691 TV is a device on which society spends billions in order to increase the total amount of ignorance.

Remember?

1692 Remember when you could dress well for what it costs now for a bikini?

Shoddy appliances

1693 Appliances are so shoddy now that when they're given as wedding presents they don't even last as long as the marriage.

Heap o' living

1694 It takes a heap o' living to make a house a home — that's paid for.

Way it goes

1695 Money doesn't come easy — but then, that's the way it goes.

Money to burn

1696 What with prices going up the way they are we'll soon have money to burn, and that's all it will be good for.

COOKING LESSONS
Charcoal
1697   I've taught my wife how to save on our barbecue expenses. She saves her toast to use as charcoal.

Creativity
1698   This course encourages your creativity. Dream up your own dishes that will be a gourmet's delight and your own excuses when they flop.

Fit for the gods
1699   When you complete this course people who taste your cooking will say, "This is food fit for the gods," without adding, "It's certainly not fit for humans."

Learning
1700   See, you're learning how to cook! Already you've learned that removing the food from the freezer will thaw it.

Cinderella
1701   Before she took our classes, her husband called her Cinderella because of the meals she served him.

COURTSHIP AND MARRIAGE LECTURE
Mind like bed
1702   A mind is like a bed: when it's all made up there's nothing in it.

Smart man
1703   A truly smart man is one who never makes others look stupid.

Heavy cross
1704   A chip on the shoulder can be a heavy cross to bear.

Good eraser
1705   Desire is a good eraser for rubbing things from the mind.

Meanderings
1706   A man who desires to reach a woman's heart should do as the water in a stream: he should not follow a direct course, but instead should indulge in all those meanderings that probe the path of least resistance.

Argument
1707   It takes two to make an argument, but only one to end it.

DEBUTS
Contributions
1708 Parents proclamation: Here are our contributions to improving our environment.

Catch a man
1709 These girls will never have to run fast to catch a man. All they'll need to do is stop running.

Pride and shame
1710 The purpose of debuts today is not to show pride in our daughters, but rather to prove we're not ashamed of them.

Transitional period
1711 A debut is the transitional period between sugar'n spice'n all that's nice and drinks'n ice'n all that rice.

Such a gift
1712 Today, as these lovely girls are presented to society, I wonder why society instead of the parents isn't paying for such a gift.

DEDICATION CEREMONIES
Solid foundation
1713 Think of the solid foundation upon which this building is constructed: the bedrock, the many tons of cement, the mortgages.

In memory
1714 Just think of the thousands of hours of mind-wearying planning and the back-breaking work, the agonizing toil and sweat that went into construction of this magnificent edifice. In memory, let us now have five minutes of sleep.

True dedication
1715 It is comparatively easy to give a speech for this dedication. The true dedication came from the men who designed and built this noble structure, but above all it will come from those who'll have to pay for it.

Wearying labors
1716 This noble edifice could only come into use through the wearying labors of myriads of bricklayers, plumbers, carpenters and other workers — and, I might add, the selfless people who must listen to dedication speeches.

A prayer

1717 This building is dedicated with the prayer that it will exist as long as its mortgage.

DEMOCRATIC CONVENTION

Poor with us

1718 The poor have always been with us. So have various forms of Republicans — and the latter explains the former.

All for little man

1719 The Republicans are all for the little man, whom they keep putting into high offices.

Party of the poor man

1720 The Republican Party is the party of the poor man. Its policy is to keep as many as possible as poor as possible.

Four-letter word

1721 "Republican" is the longest four-letter word in our language.

Positive

1722 I believe in giving positive suggestions: Thrash the scoundrels!

Lot on their side

1723 If the Republicans win the next election it's because they have a lot on their side, namely millions of dupes.

DENTISTS MEETINGS

Sweet tooth

1724 Talk about a sweet tooth! He brushes his teeth with a lollipop.

Bigmouths

1725 This is the only profession in which the practitioners are glad to meet a bunch of bigmouths.

Gold in your pocket

1726 Putting gold in your clients' teeth when they don't need it can put it in your pocket — but let's keep their teeth and our reputations white.

Experts at repair

1727 Make yourselves experts at repair. Better a filled cavity in a tooth than an empty one in the gum.

Bill collecting

1728 As we all know, bill collecting can be quite a problem. One can get bitten trying to repossess a filling.

Seller's market

1729 Ours is a seller's market — but if you want to feel really secure, buy some sugar stock.

DOCTORS MEETINGS

Doctors work hard

1730 We doctors work hard to help our patients live long and productive lives. That's the only way our bills will be paid.

Born Free?

1731 Obstetricians are now being accused of trying to ban the song "Born Free."

Hello

1732 We must now decide the fee that should be charged our patients for saying Hello.

30,000 medicines

1733 Doesn't it bother you that there are at least 30,000 medicines in the modern pharmecopeia, and you have tried only 20,000 of them?

Repairmen

1734 Surely we have the right to charge a lot, like other repairmen.

Friend of labor

1735 *Obstetrician:* a friend of labor.

ECOLOGISTS MEETINGS

Clean air

1736 Things have changed. Today we say, "Lets have some clean air — close the window."

Furnace cleaners

1737 Air pollution could yet be a boon to someone — perhaps to furnace cleaners, who might be used for cleaning out people's lungs.

SST noise

1738   The noise from an SST would not be entirely bad. In the wilderness it might drown out the sound from off-road vehicles.

Oasis

1739   An oasis in the desert used to be a spot blessed with water. Today it's one without litter.

Walk on water

1740   Before long all of us will be able to walk on water. Not because we'll be sufficiently pure, but because the water will be sufficiently polluted.

Unlike weather

1741   Unlike weather, pollution is something people not only talk about — they contribute to it as well.

Lifeless desert

1742   Now that men have landed on the moon they'll soon turn it into a lifeless desert.

ELECTION CAMPAIGN SPEECH
Fool the people

1743   My opponent keeps running because he believes that, while it's true you can't fool all of the people all of the time, he only needs a majority.

Best speech

1744   My opponent received an award for making the best speech of 1870.

Honesty in government

1745   My opponent must believe in honesty in government. Why else would he let us know what a fool he is?

Heart of a maiden

1746   My opponent has yet to learn that an election is like the heart of a maiden: it cannot be bought, it must be won.

Keep my promises to myself

1747   I will not promise more than I can deliver. Therefore I will keep my promises — to myself.

Etching-retching
1748 I shall make my outline brief lest my etching deserve a retching.

People misunderstand
1749 My trouble is that people misunderstand my opponent. They think he is not as bad as he seems.

ELECTION VICTORY SPEECH
Desire and challenge
1750 It is now my desire and challenge to see that my constituents benefit more from my getting into office than they have done by the fact that my opponent did not.

To the victor
1751 Since this office was held so long by the opposition, I can only say that that well-known statement should now be revised to say, "To the victor goes the spoiled."

A kiss
1752 I thank you for your unstinting efforts and in gratitude throw you, instead of bull, a kiss.

Not the voters' loss
1753 This victory tonight could have happened to a better man, but not to a more fortunate man — one who had the support of people like you. I will now work to make certain that my victory is not the voters' loss.

Not have to run
1754 I ran for this office. Now I promise to so conduct myself that I'll not have to run when I leave it.

An honest man
1755 We do honor tonight to the victor. The best man won but the voters won more — an honest man. His victory proves that he was sold but he can never be bought.

EMPLOYER'S SPEECH TO EMPLOYEES
Don't accomplish anything
1756 Perhaps it's justified for you to malinger and visit on the job After all, you don't accomplish anything when you're working.

Profit by mistakes

1757 There's really an easier way for you to get rich. Learn to profit by your mistakes.

Efficient employee

1758 Now here's a really efficient employee. He wastes 100 percent of the time possible.

Good liar

1759 John got the day off for a very good reason. The reason is, he's a good liar.

Working conditions

1760 Mary quit her job because of the working conditions here. We told her that work was one of the conditions of her employment.

Transfer

1761 If you wish to keep your job you may have to accept a transfer — to Deadwood City.

FAMILY REUNIONS

Public relations

1762 Now let's give a big vote of thanks to the organizer who made this reunion possible. You might say that he's a promoter of public relations.

Common ancestor

1763 All of us descended from a common ancestor who was anything but common.

Old family tree

1764 Hooray for the old family tree, the one thing that will make all of us hang together! Oops! I mean the one thing that will make us stick together.

Why they avoid relatives

1765 A family reunion is a place where most people go once a year to remind themselves of why they avoid relatives. But we've got a good bunch of folks.

Would not be here

1766 I salute our common ancestor, without whom we would not be here with each other today or be alive to regret it.

FATHERS AND SONS OUTINGS

Living proof

1767 Boys, we fathers are very bright. You're the living proof of it!

Hurts me

1768 Boys, when we spank you it truly hurts us more than it does you. We have arthritis.

Let grass grow

1769 We've found that you boys never let any grass grow under feet — after we plant a new lawn.

Lipstick

1770 I see that you boys still have the color of youth on your cheeks. Lipstick.

Disheartening

1771 It's very disheartening. We fathers work hard for our boys; we sacrifice and raise them the very best we know how, and then they turn out to be like us.

Shaw was wrong

1772 George Bernard Shaw was wrong. Youth isn't wasted on you.

Incompetent

1773 We suspect that you boys sometimes want to say: "We respect our elders. We admire them for being able to stay alive so long when they're so darned incompetent."

FATHER'S DAY SPEECH

Still a good man

1774 Dad, you don't wear long hair, skin-tight pants or weird hairdos, but you're still a good man to me. Happy Father's Day!

Prejudiced

1775 I don't want to be prejudiced just because you're my father. So I'll be prejudiced because you're a great father.

Wonderful genes

1776 Dad, I think you have wonderful genes. I couldn't live without them.

Come from Heaven

1777 Children must come from Heaven because I have a Heavenly Father.

Good luck
1778   Why oh why was I ever born to you? Just good luck I guess.

Good parent
1779   I've given up trying to be a good son. Now I just want to be a good father like you.

Perfect father
1780   You're such a perfect father that I wouldn't even mind having you as an in-law.

Heart belongs to daddy
1781   The doctor took my tonsils, the dentist has my teeth, and I haven't paid for my wig. But my heart belongs to daddy.

FUNERAL EULOGIES
Needs no headstone
1782   The deceased needs no headstone. He is his own monument and memorial.

Life attests his worth
1783   It is not fitting that we praise the deceased. His life attests to his worth far more than words can do. So I shall give an account of his days here on earth, as he can be proud to do to the Lord.

Any friend he pleased
1784   He could have any friend he pleased, and he pleased everyone.

New star
1785   There may not have been a new star in the heavens on the night he was born, but there certainly was here on earth.

Rare souls
1786   His epitaph should read: "Here lies one of those rare souls who will enrich heaven."

Man so modest
1787   The departed was a man so modest that he would be embarrassed by all that has been said today, but so percipient as to know its truth.

GRADUATION EXERCISES
Abundant experience

1788   It is a base canard to say that university students get no experience which suits them for the business world. They get abundant experience at cheating.

Do their thing

1789   As we turn these students out into the world to do their thing, let's hope there are enough police to handle it.

Fine group

1790   This group of students is as fine as you'll see anywhere. Other colleges are having their problems, too.

Drip

1791   *Drip:* One who's dropped out.

Whew!

1792   Ladies and gentlemen, on this graduation day as we turn your children back to you, I'm sure that I speak for all of the teachers as well as myself when I say, clearly and sincerely, "Whew!"

New vices

1793   Our youth is very inventive. It has dreamed up many new vices.

Youth's turn

1794   Our generation has controlled the world and failed. Now let's give youth its turn — to muck it up.

HEALTH LECTURE
Carry to the grave

1795   There are those who make fun of our interest in health foods. And when we fail to convince them, they carry their prejudices right into the grave.

Good advice

1796   I know one health lecturer who had a bald head, pockmarks, and an obese body. But we should not ignore the advice of even such a one, because he could say, as Mr. Micawber said to David Copperfield, "My advice must be good. Because I didn't take it, and look at me."

Lung cancer scare

1797 The lung cancer scare frightened people so much they had to increase their cigarette consumption to quiet their nerves.

Working out

1798 Feel my arm. I've been working out on the bars — the chocolate bars.

Bitter pills

1799 Your health should come from nutritional food and not from bitter pills. In line with that, I'll try to see that this speech does not become one of the latter.

INSPIRATIONAL SPEECHES

Wise man

1800 It's a wise man who isn't a know-it-all.

Walked upon

1801 There is no sh' ie in being walked upon. The shame comes if one lies down instead of being knocked down.

Sell his soul

1802 The more prone is a man to sell his soul, the less is its worth.

Don't be afraid

1803 Don't be afraid of tomorrow — it's always a day away.

Big head

1804 A big head is a lot of weight to carry on your shoulders.

Chin-ups

1805 The best exercise for the depressed is chin-ups.

Something we ain't

1806 We're so busy trying to be something we ain't that we've got no time to improve what we are.

True honesty

1807 True honesty is priceless. It can't be bought at any price.

Stiff neck

1808 If you must have a stiff neck, make it one that keeps you not only from looking up to anyone but also from looking down on others.

INTRODUCTION SPEECH

The greatest

1809 All I can say about the man I am about to introduce is that he's the greatest. Anything less and he'll have my job.

Best known

1810 And now I'd like to introduce our most famous and unforgettable, best-known speaker: — Uh, pardon me, what is your name?

Far more praise

1811 A wise man would never praise our speaker. His endeavors and accomplishments say far more in his praise than any elocutionist ever could.

Fool's-eye view

1812 And now to give us a fool's-eye view of the situation, here is our speaker . . .

His opinion

1813 Our speaker can hardly wait to get out here and state his opinion so *he'll* know what it is.

INVENTORS CONFERENCE

Flash of genius

1814 If you are fortunate enough to have a flash of genius, just hope that you can make it last longer than a flash.

No compensation

1815 I think that many of us inventors are finding that inventing is a small part inspiration, a large part perspiration, and no compensation.

Made men rich

1816 The patent system opened an unparalleled era of inventiveness that made many men rich — namely, those patent brokers, lawyers, searchers, etc. who prey on the gullible inventor.

Things to be invented

Let's add to the list of things to be invented:

1817   A television set without knobs.

A television set that tunes in nothing but commercials, since they are better than the shows.

Brandy-flavored lipstick (doubles the appeal to men).

A miniskirt that can be let down to be as large as a bikini.

Powered door slammers for kids.

Powered hand clapper.

Businessmen inventors

1818   All inventors are not businessmen but most businessmen are inventors, when it comes to keeping books for Internal Revenue purposes.

Loose screw

1819   Did you hear the one about the inventor who walked into the psychiatrist's office leading a mechanical man by the hand and said, "Doc, I want you to help Roton here. He's got a screw loose somewhere."

LECTURES (GENERAL)

Van Gogh

1820   Though I know you are not Van Goghs, I say to you, "Fellow countrymen, lend me your ear!"

Seismograph office

1821   My knees are causing consternation in the seismograph office.

Gone with the breeze

1822   In closing let me just say, "Lest I seem too windy, I shall be gone with the breeze."

Not profitable

1823   Lecturing is not a profitable profession; in fact, the most affluent lecturer I know is one who is so bad he's paid not to speak.

Closing prayer

1824   I shall now end this sermon before you listeners give a closing prayer.

Better than it sounds

1825 I sincerely hope that it will not be said of my speech what Mark Twain said about a p rticular kind of music: "It's better than it sounds."

Captive audience

1826 The goal of some lecturers is that of most professors, namely to have a captive audience. I too desire a captive audience, but I want my audience to be captured by what I say.

LIBERALS RALLY

Base lie

1827 Some people say that our legislators do nothing but sit and twiddle their thumbs. This is a base lie. Oh, if only it weren't!

The only truth

1828 The only truth that ever comes out of a trial is that the truth never comes out of a trial.

Medieval history

1829 My college friend wants to teach medieval history. Conservatives want to make it.

Republican credo

1830 The Republican credo is: The Democrats have given you a false prosperity. Let us give you a real poverty.

Lithic-ific

1831 Republicans — Paleolithic
Communists — Monolithic
Democrats — Terrific

Taxes on the rich

1832 No president can be expected to lower taxes on the rich. They don't pay any now.

MEMORIAL DAY SPEECH

Into the grave

1833 It is our fervent hope that the day is soon approaching when we can put war into the grave along with its victims.

Fought and died

1834   Our honored war dead have fought and died for our way of
life, namely fighting and dying.

War to end all wars

1835   Let us all work to see that an atomic war is not the only way
to have a war to end all wars.

Did not die in vain

1836   Memorial Day was established in the hope that our brave soldiers did not die in vain. The floral tributes before us, and the
florists' profits they represent, attest to the fact they didn't.

Wrap in a flag

1837   We wrap our war dead in a flag. Those responsible for their
deaths wrap themselves in a flag.

MODERATOR

Moderation

1838   I shall try to be unobtrusive, for my motto is, "Moderation in
all things, including moderation.

Gauze mask

1839   One of my functions as a moderator for this group is that of
a gauze mask in relation to germs and people, namely to keep
them from each other's throats.

Good hot water system

1840   An ideal moderator might be said to resemble an efficient
hot water heating system. He keeps things warm but never lets
them get too hot, he restricts pollutants, and he uses radiation
instead of hot air.

Two to make an argument

1841   It takes two to make an argument but only one to end it — the
moderator.

Back and forth

1842   Remember, panelists, you are to throw ideas back and forth.
But please try to do so as ballplayers and not as cannons.

MOTHERS AND DAUGHTERS OUTINGS

Admirable daughters

1843   We mothers don't ask that you girls become like us, only that
you have daughters as admirable as those we mothered.

Failures

1844 Why should children respect their parents when their parents have been such failures that they've raised kids who don't respect them?

Resentment

1845 We mothers resent the age of teenagers and they resent ours. It would be nice if we could split the difference.

Hiding

1846 We've sometimes felt that if our daughters ever came out of hiding, that's what they were going to get. But today makes us feel proud of them.

Flypaper

1847 Perhaps one way of making our daughters useful is to utilize their hands as flypaper.

Togetherness

1848 These outings afford our mothers and daughters a little togetherness other than at dishwashing time.

MOTHER'S DAY SPEECH

Rib

1849 Mother, I don't mind your being a rib.
It makes you closer to my heart.

Lamb

1850 Mother, I just want to tell you you're a lamb. And that's no bull.

Fortune

1851 Everyone must have a mother, but only great good fortune gave me you.

Mum

1852 What is loving, kind, considerate, honest and unselfish? Mum's the word.

Maxi-mum

1853 I wish you the maxi-mum. You're the most.

Judge by the fruit

1854 If it's true that you can judge a tree by the fruit it bears, you're a great mother. Thanks for bearing so much.

Lie about other things

1855   Mother, you're not the sweetest, kindest, gentlest mother in the world. (And I lie about other things, too.)

Lottery

1856   There must have been a lottery for mothers in the life before this — and I won.

Ford Foundation

1857   Mother, if love were money, you'd be the Ford Foundation.

NEW YEAR'S EVE PARTY

Party's over

1858   In closing, let me say that the party's over and I shall no longer beat your ear-drums.

Year older

1859   Do you feel a year older, now that the New Year is here? When you get out of bed in the morning you'll feel twenty years older.

Spanking

1860   We're supposed to drink a toast to that jovial infant who brings in the New Year. Why? He seems to carry a load of land mines in that diaper of his. If the next New Year is as bad as the last, I'm going to give him a spanking.

You've come a long way

1861   Which of us can look back on last year's New Year's Eve — the beginning symbol of this year — and say, "Baby, you've come a long way?"

Joyous year

1862   Toast: May each and every one of you find that all of the coming year is as joyous as this party, and not its hangover.

Respect old age

1863   Why do we celebrate the infancy of the new year instead of the old age of the last? We're supposed to respect old age. Oh, that's it: we respect the behavioral age of the revelers.

PANEL DISCUSSIONS

Ten Einsteins

1864   Critics of panel discussions say that ten mediocre minds aren't as good as one Einstein. But to an intellectual, ten Einsteins are better than one, just as to a beer drinker ten steins are better than ein.

Gift of tongues

1865   Having a group like this instead of a single speaker gives us the gift of tongues.

Flint and tinder

1866   And now, panelists, be like flint and tinder: let there be friction, let there be sparks, let there be heat, and let there be light.

Immoral

1867   Let this group prove by its discussion that not all groupies are immoral.

Not wooden

1868   We'll bear in mind that, though this is a panel discussion, it doesn't have to be wooden.

Grand opening

1869   Listen to the great words emanate from his mouth. Listen for the grand opening.

PEP TALKS

Peaceful demonstration

1870   Boys, you can beat that team! Just get out and charge them, kick them, thrash them, commit mayhem — in short, just pretend you're having a peaceful campus demonstration.

Kid brother

1871   Just remember that that team out there is no better than you are. They make just as many mistakes, they're just as vulnerable, they're no brighter or stronger. Come to think of it, why don't I just send my kid brother out to beat them?

Hope of the future

1872　Doesn't it make you teenagers despair to think that *you* are the hope of the future?

How to win

1873　It's true that the primary reason you come to college is to learn, but sports is to teach you how to win.

PERSONALITY IMPROVEMENT TALK

Raiment

1874　Clothe your emotions in gorgeous raiment — a smile.

Gift of gab

1875　The gift of gab is knowing when to shut up.

Coincidence

1876　Is it just coincidence that the mouth is bigger than the ear?

Feeling important

1877　Nothing is as important as feeling important.

Like a radio

1878　A good person is like a good radio. He has good reception, high fidelity, can have his tune changed, and doesn't make a lot of noise when turned down.

Face you save

1879　When it comes to pride, make sure the face you save is worth saving.

PHILOSOPHY SPEECH

Wisdom tooth

1880　A wisdom tooth is the one that never bites off more than it can chew.

Improbable

1881　Nothing is impossible, but everything is improbable.

Stopped clock

1882　Nothing is all wrong. Even a stopped clock is right twice a day.

Doctor of Philosophy

1883　He's a Doctor of Philosophy. He doctors philosophy.

The quest

1884 In love as in life we get our kicks
Not from the carrots but from the sticks.
In plainer words, that that's best
Is not the goal but rather the quest.

High standard

1885 Americans are people with a high standard of living and low standards for living.

Reason

1886 Reason should be used as a tool, not a weapon.

Different angles

1887 Thinking should be like the eyes. Depth is provided by seeing things from different angles.

POETRY READINGS

Meanderings

1888 As we take our journey into poetry, may my mellifluous meanderings be tortuous but never torturous.

Poetic license

1889 I told one group that I use poetic license and someone in the audience remarked that in my case it should never have been granted.

Rhyme or reason

1890 I've tried not to put rhyme or reason in my poetry, only feeling and emotion.

Difficult chore

1891 The most difficult chore for a poet is to make sure that when the muses stir him, he doesn't become all mixed up.

POLICE RALLY

Bluecoat

1892 When it comes to crime, be glad you're a bluecoat instead of a turncoat.

Rights

1893 They're soon going to send lawyers around with policemen to advise the policemen of their rights.

Reformatory

1894 A reformatory is an institution dedicated to the belief that a hitch in time saves nine.

Spank it

1895 If I were able to take the law into my own hands, I'd spank it.

College students

1896 The more we see of college students these days, the more of them we find revolting.

Plainclothesmen

1897 Many of us are plainclothesmen. That doesn't necessarily mean detectives; with our salaries, we have no choice.

POLITICAL RALLIES

Tricky

1898 He's so tricky he even fooled himself — he really believed he wouldn't run again.

Doesn't change

1899 My opponent is a man who doesn't change his stands. He doesn't know what they are.

Honest thing

1900 Recently I heard my opponent say, "I'll be damned!" Only honest thing he's ever said.

Despotism

1901 Vote for my opponent and make our country free for despotism.

Nation's fools

1902 My opponent's election proves there are many intelligent men in this country. All of them predicted the nation's fools would elect the next president.

Sweep the city

1903 It's possible that my opponent will sweep the city — if the sanitation department will hire him.

Aiding the enemy

1904 Anyone who demonstrates against the incumbent is aiding the enemy. They win sympathy for him and help him into office again.

PSYCHOLOGISTS (Discussions about)
Profitable
1905   Psychologists apparently find it more profitable to cure others.

Husband and psychiatrist
1906   The difference between a husband and a psychiatrist is that the husband must pay to listen to his wife instead of getting paid. Of course, the psychiatrist must pretend to listen.

Disrobe
1907   Psychologists disrobe your psyche and show your knock-knees.

Not normal
1908   Among the people she runs with, you're not normal if you don't go to a psychiatrist.

I.Q. test
1909   Two psychologists watch a cat at a table, writing. One psychologist says to the other, "I'm giving him an I.Q. test to see if he's smart."

P.T.A. MEETINGS
TV
1910   The way things are going, the only ABC's our grandchildren will know is a TV network.

More learning
1911   There needs to be more learning. And now let's swear we're going to learn it.

Salary position
1912   As parents, we do understand you teachers' salary position. You merely want to earn as much as we give our children for an allowance.

In common
1913   What unites us as parents and teachers is that we have the children in common and want to make them uncommon.

Respect
1914   Our children should respect us. After all, they can see that we have produced a generation superior to us, and let them be humbled by the fact that they will do the same.

Night out

1915 Attending a P.T.A. meeting is the only way the boys can get a night out.

PUBLISHERS CONVENTION

Progress

1916 There has indeed been progress in freedom of the press. Today we only burn the books and not the authors.

New records

1917 One of our new books is setting unprecedented records. It's being unread by more people than any other book in publishing history.

Rags to riches

1918 There's a publisher who has gone from rags to riches by printing only the rags.

Novelist-novelty

1919 As you know, a novelist is one who writes book-length fiction. A novelty, as you also know, is one who writes *good* book-length fiction.

Publish and perish

1920 Considering the writing ability of some of our college authors, the rule should be "Publish and perish."

Plot

1921 The story plot of many authors seems to be directed against the publishers.

Mess media

1922 Apparently that author reads the mess media.

RADICALS RALLY

Non-Communists

1923 That right-wing organization has a file that lists the names of all the people in the United States who are not Communists.

Wisdom

1924 Wisdom is a quality that's venerated and overrated.

Congress

1925 It's a rump Congress — full of asses.

Lend your ears

1926 Fellow countrymen, lend me your ears. We've already got your shirt.

Russian roulette

1927 No, the voters didn't flip a coin when they elected that man. They played Russian roulette with the nation and lost.

Perverts

1928 The army won't accept perverts. It wants its killers to have high morals.

Lives dangerously

1929 He lives dangerously — he says what he thinks.

REPUBLICAN CONVENTION

Good word

1930 Now let me say a good word for Democrats: Republicans.

Love, leave

1931 If you don't love this country, leave it. If you do love it, vote Republican.

Premeditated crime

1932 We'll have to forgive those who voted Democratic. While this vote was a premeditated crime, it wasn't done with malice.

No right to complain

1933 You have no right to complain about your government if you didn't bother to vote, or if you voted Democratic.

Helping the nation

1934 If the Democrats in Congress really believed in getting out and helping the nation, that's what they'd do — get out.

Right thing

1935 We must admit the Democrats are honest. They wouldn't do the right thing even if you bribed them.

RETIREMENT CEREMONY OR PARTY

Wise

1936 They say that age brings wisdom. But you have honored me so much tonight on my retirement that if I'd been wise I'd have retired long before now.

Retiring personality

1937   I've been told I have a retiring personality. Now's my chance to find out if it's true.

Boon

1938   Retirement is a boon granted by society to those in their autumn years so that they will have to attend the funerals of their friends, which usually occur at 2 p.m. on working days.

Priceless gift

1939   Every retiree receives a priceless gift — his freedom.

Declining years

1940   Old age is called the declining years because of all the good things one has to decline.

Retirement present

1941   For many years I've worked and slaved for a retirement present — enough money to retire.

REVIVAL MEETING

Cremation

1942   Cremation is acclimatization for the next life.

Blazes

1943   What in the blazes are you going to be doing in the next life?

Die happy

1944   Everyone should die happy. After all, they're leaving this world behind.

Thank God

1945   Thank God! Think God!

Really lived

1946   Many religious people believe that you haven't really lived until you've died.

Pray for help

1947   Don't be like the man who won't pray for help with his troubles because he believes they're too much, even for the Lord.

SAFETY MEETING OR LECTURE

Watch out

1948 When you drive, watch out for little children. One of them may be driving the car next to you.

Eye on road

1949 Keep your eye on the road — but watch the other cars, too.

Gassed

1950 Many accidents occur when the car and driver are both gassed.

Turn for hearse

1951 Don't drive too fast around curves or you may be taking a turn for the hearse.

To heaven fast

1952 Many people seem determined to get to heaven just as fast as their cars will take them.

Safety college

1953 A hospital might be termed a college that teaches safety consciousness.

Cigarettes

1954 Cigarettes burn smokers. Cigarette smoking burns non-smokers.

SALES MEETINGS

Hard knocks

1955 Door to door selling: school of hard knocks.

Anything right

1956 I'd be the last to say you can't ever do anything right. I only say you don't.

Sales figures

1957 The most important sales figures for any company are its best salesmen.

Lousy salesman

1958 Talk about a lousy salesman! He couldn't even sell life insurance in a terminal ward.

Eskimos

1959 The salesman we want is the kind who can sell refrigerators to Eskimos by offering sunsuits as premiums.

Shabby products

1960 Salesmen, sell yourselves — no shabby products!

SCHOOL LECTURES

Matter of degree

1961 Many a school dropout has discovered that success is all a matter of degree.

Why?

1962 When he was a child his teacher would phone his mother, wanting to know why he *was* in school.

Concentration camp

1963 Library: concentration camp

Speed talking course

1964 Our greatest educational need is a speed talking course, to teach people how to say what they have to say in one percent of the time it now requires.

Educational television

1965 Educational television is one that's turned off.

Working class

1966 Teacher to new group: You are now members of the working class.

Union building

1967 Student union building: a place where students may go to forget the lessons they never learned.

SCOUT MEETINGS

Old Ladies

1968 Our boys don't help old ladies across the street by sounding a loud car horn in their ears.

Good behavior

1969 You've been exemplary boys, so I'm giving you some time off for good behavior.

Hurts

1970 Our boys tell the truth even when it hurts — themselves, not someone else.

New item

1971 Some of our boys have asked that we add a new item to our camping list — a hair net.

Good deed

1972 Scouts, you should do a good deed every day. For example, you might help your mother clean the dishes — and that means more than just eating the food on them.

Courtesy

1973 Scouts, start living up to your reputations for courtesy. If each one of you was to begin helping old ladies across the street every day, they would no longer be struck down by autos; on the other hand, they might end up in the hospital from shock.

Great things

1974 We parents wish great things for our boys. We want them to be honest, upright, moral and so on, but if they can't achieve that we want them to be like us.

SPORTS BANQUET

Faith

1975 We had faith in you boys. We knew you'd win. Still, we didn't hire the dishwashers until we were absolutely sure.

Shared honor

1976 The athletes we honor here tonight deserve all the accolades they receive. But in fairness they should share these with the pep team. We all know how those girls drove our team to victory with all those brightly colored pompoms, green pills, red pills, yellow pills. . .

Vile potation

1977 The wonderful athletes we honor tonight exemplify clean, moral, healthful living. So in toasting them, let us now drink this vile, alcoholic potation.

Not the winning

1978   It's not the winning, it's how you play the game that counts. But if you lose, then obviously you didn't know how to play the game.

Congratulations

1979   I now wish to read this fulsome letter of congratulations to our successful team: "Greetings... From your friendly Internal Revenue Service."

STOCKHOLDERS MEETING

Portfolio

1980   Your choice portfolio illustrates well the lesson that, in business as in your personal life, the greatest rewards come to those who keep the right company.

Dividends

1981   We're pleased to see so many stockholders in attendance. We know you hope that your interest as well as this company will pay you dividends.

Let's face it

1982   Gentlemen, let's face it: our principal interest is interest on our principal.

Indices are up

1983   All of the major business indices are up — employment, sales, prices... losses.

Bore

1984   Our losses are like a bore — even though we try to ignore them, they won't go away.

SUCCESS TALKS

Boat

1985   A boat that isn't being rocked isn't moving.

Dead weight

1986   He who doesn't rock the boat is nought but dead weight.

Love of self

1987   Love of self precedes greatness as often as it follows it.

Positive thinking

1988 The power of positive thinking is proved by all the money extracted by the writers about it from the believers in it.

Advice

1989 Advice on getting rich: Don't take any advice.

On the ball

1990 The man who is on the ball can roll right along in this life.

Opportunity

1991 Make sure that when opportunity knocks there's someone home.

SUNDAY SCHOOL LESSONS

No!

1992 When their date's fangs show... The girls who know, No!

Iceberg

1993 A woman is not necessarily an iceberg just because she leaves most of her body unexposed.

Soft soap

1994 Soft soap won't wash clean the girls who buy it.

Virtue will win

1995 Some say that righteousness will never prevail,
And that mankind is all going to hell.
But there's a way for virtue to win:
Just convince everybody that it's really sin.

Ten Commandments

1996 I keep the Ten Commandments. They're home in my drawer.

Stainless steal

1997 There's no such thing as a stainless steal.

Supreme justice

1998 Yes, there is a supreme justice. Good or bad, a man deservedly is forced to live with himself.

TAXPAYERS MEETING

Lazy people

1999 I never resented paying taxes until I realized they were being used to pay people as lazy as I.

Property

2000 Recently I noticed some signs on several boxes saying "Property of Internal Revenue." How redundant, I thought: everything is.

High taxes

2001 The reason for high taxes that government levies
Is that we insist on Cads instead of Chevies.

Ward of state

2002 A ward of the state is what a man becomes after paying his taxes.

The trouble

2003 The trouble with supporting our government is that we don't get to shop around before we put down our taxes.

TEACHERS CONVENTION

Third degree

2004 Doctoral exams: the third degree for the third degree.

"A" student

2005 An "A" student is one who is trying — especially to those who don't get A's.

Inspirations

2006 All of us teachers stand as inspirations to our students — not to become teachers unless they want to be overworked and underpaid.

Bad grade

2007 Just make sure that if you must give a pupil a bad grade it isn't the one he's in.

Work all year

2008 There's a movement underway to have us work all year around with a commensurate raise. At least that sounds better than what we're doing — working nine months and receiving six months' pay.

TEMPERANCE SPEECH

Fluid drive

2009 It's axiomatic that a hydromatic
Is a form of fluid drive.

But it's even truer, you'll find no doer
Seeking fluid drive in a dive.

Best hedge

2010 The best hedge against inflation and going broke is to let any bottle of whiskey you buy mature for years and then sell it.

Pressurized bottles

2011 Why not pressurize liquor bottles so the contents will come out faster?

Recycling

2012 Recycling can be carried too far. For example, an alcoholic recently suffocated when he put a plastic bag over his head, hoping to recycle his breath.

Insect

2013 The most ubiquitous and inimical species of the insect world is the barfly.

Sober

2014 Drinking makes the drinker drunk, and so it should make us sober.

Safety belt

2015 Safety belt: the one you don't drink.

TESTIMONIAL DINNERS

No more

2016 But let us laud this man no more, lest he fear he is attending not a testimonial dinner but his own funeral.

Thank the waiters

2017 Let us give thanks to the waiters for their excellent service. Unlike some I have known, they have not served drinks upon all.

Great Circle Route

2018 In honoring our friend tonight I won't travel the Great Circle Route. I'll talk directly and just say, "He's a great guy!"

Extolled

2019 The previous speakers have extolled our guest of honor so expansively that I'd like to receive the same tributes by becoming such a great man myself.

Jealousy

2020   The sincerest testimonial the man we honor can have is that we here do not dislike him. Anyone else of such illustrious accomplishments ordinarily would know the hatred that stems from jealousy.

THANKSGIVING DINNERS
Self-basting turkey

2021   One of the latest new products is a Thanksgiving turkey that bastes itself in Pepto-Bismol.

Gobblers

2022   This Thanksgiving dinner is so delicious that there's more than one gobbler at the table.

Not enough

2023   Unfortunately, thanks is not enough to assure grace. Indians celebrated the first Thanksgiving, and look at what happened to them.

Prayer

2024   I wonder what kind of prayer turkeys give on Thanksgiving.

Full hearts

2025   After such an engorging feast, may our hearts be filled with thanksgiving and our stomachs with Alka Seltzer.

TOASTMASTER
Handle his liquor

2026   I learned today the origin of the word "toastmaster." It means one who is able to handle his liquor.

Lot of crap

2027   A toastmaster is one who is no dice player but who shoots a lot of crap.

Going to slip

2028   I've been told that, as a toastmaster, one of these times I'm going to slip on my own ooze.

Breakfast cereals

2029   A master of ceremonies should be like certain breakfast cereals in some ways and not in others. That is, he should have snap, crackle and pop, and never become soggy, but he shouldn't be made of corn.

Bitter mood

2030 When I'm in an especially bitter mood I feel that I have an appropriate word for every occasion — Damn!

TOASTS

One life

2031 To a prominent citizen: He is such a useful citizen that I regret he has but one life to live for his country.

How good are you

2032 To a saintly person: We're all aware of how good you are, so all I can say is, will you let me hold on to your feet when you ascend?

Roasted

2033 Though I've never been toasted by anyone, I've been roasted.

Mighty big words

2034 Splendiferous, effulgent, decorous, circumspect, grandiloquent, magnanimous, articulate, erudite, impeccable, unimpeachable, luminous, sagacious, salubrious... It takes some mighty big words to describe you.

Righteous

2035 To a modest man, who would have us believe he has spent his life doing good deeds just to deceive us into believing he is righteous.

TRAFFIC EXPERTS CONVENTION

Bumper crop

2036 America has a bumper crop each year — a million pedestrians injured annually.

Courage

2037 It's commonly said, of course, that you shouldn't drink if you're going to drive. But with so many terrible drivers on the road, how else can one summon up the courage?

What's driving

2038 We have so many car accidents not because of what's driving the cars, but mostly because of what's driving the drivers.

Fools and angels

2039   Fools rush where angels too have sped.

Man who gets your girl

2040   Keep your eyes on the road, your hands on the wheel, and your mind on driving. Then maybe you'll outlive the man who gets your girl.

Demons

2041   I oftentimes think that cars and their drivers are driven by demons.

Clean highways

2042   "Keep our highways clean."
         What the writers mean:
         If you must collide,
         Do it at the side.

TRAINING LECTURE
Everything I know

2043   In this course I'll teach you everything I know. Then, to fill the other 90 percent of the time, I'll assign you textbooks to read.

Teaching assistant

2044   The best teaching assistant is a smart student.

Know your teacher

2045   Students, learn your lessons to the letter.
         But for an "A," know your teacher better.

TRAVEL AGENTS CONVENTION
Hardships

2046   An American tourist is one who likes to tell of all his hardships in darkest Africa when actually the lights went out for two hours in his Hilton Hotel room.

Explorers

2047   Quite a few people want to visit the unexplored areas of the world but don't do it because they can't find detailed guidebooks and there aren't enough Howard Johnson's.

Cook's tour

2048 Let us compliment the chef for that exotic cuisine which took us on such a delightful cook's tour.

Remote places

2049 Americans like to travel to exotic, remote, hard-to-get-to places with a new Hilton and jet runway.

Diseases

2050 Yes, there are many diseases in some of the countries our American tourists visit. If they weren't already there, our clients make certain they soon are.

TRAVELOGUE

Typical tourist

2051 A typical tourist is one who doesn't want to be considered a tourist.

Enjoy what you see

2052 Advice to travelers: Don't spend too much time on pictures. Enjoy what you are seeing. Don't wait to get home before you see what you saw.

The other side

2053 Our pioneer forefathers always wanted to see what was on the other side of the hill. Today we don't even wonder what's on the other side of the billboards.

Liar

2054 I knew one traveler who was such a liar I didn't believe him when he said hello. But I'll try to stick with the truth.

UNION MEETING

Skeleton crew

2055 That employer maintains only a skeleton crew at his business. What he pays his workers doesn't maintain any more than skeletons.

Long hours and low pay

2056 All of your hard work hasn't brought you a fraction of the wages and good working conditions just your being unionized has done. You erased the memories of long hours and low pay not with booze but with your dues.

Stink

2057 That employer is airing his plans for us, but aired or not they still stink.

Good, hard work

2058 Most wealthy men have made their money from good, hard work — their employees'.

Labor Day

2059 We celebrate the high honor that goes with labor by declaring a day of rest.

The way to prestige

2060 We're proud of what we do for a living. And we don't need any stiff-collared intellectuals telling us the way to prestige is a bleach to turn our collars from blue to white.

Live or die

2061 What with the high price of doctors and funerals, we can't afford to live or die.

WEDDING ANNIVERSARIES

Seal of approval

2062 To my wife, who cleans, cooks, baby tends, dusts, mops, washes dishes, does the laundry, etc. and etc. — you have my good housekeeping seal of approval.

Best years

2063 In giving me the best years of your life, dear, you've given me mine.

Not wasted

2064 Our love is unlike youth. It's not wasted on the young.

Flat on my face

2065 If I tried to tell you what I think of you I'd fall flat on my face. That's the only thing that's appropriate.

Great advantage

2066 One indisputably great advantage to being a man is that you're a woman.

Plural marriage

2067 I believe in plural marriage — I want to marry you again and again.

WEDDING OR ENGAGEMENT SHOWERS

Too good to be true

2068 A wife who is too good to be true is one who isn't too bad to be true.

I do

2069 When a woman says "I do," that shouldn't have to last for time and eternity; she should be allowed a little more talk.

Trainer

2070 Word of advice: Be a trainer, but not a sparring partner.

Stalemate

2071 A stalemate is one you've lived with for a week.

Do what you want

2072 Always remember that you can do what you want, when you please — your husband.

WEDDINGS

Don't agree

2073 To keep your wife from constantly changing her mind, just say you don't agree with her.

Answer to prayer

2074 There is an answer to prayer! You.

See the bride

2075 Young man, it's bad luck for a groom to see his bride before the wedding. It's even worse for him to see her afterwards.

Wedding bells

2076 Wedding bells are gongs that tell the contestants to come out of their corners.

Sentence is pronounced

2077 A wedding is the ceremony at which the sentence is pronounced. The trial follows.

Rejoice

2078 Being best man at a wedding is cause for rejoicing. It means you aren't the groom.

More expensive

2079 If weddings keep getting more expensive it will soon cost as much to get married as to get divorced. This is wrong, since we always want a divorce more than a marriage.

Why?

2080 Why is it always the mothers who cry at a wedding when it should be the groom?

WOMEN'S LIB SPEECH

Grain of salt

2081 When a man makes advances to a girl, she should take him with a grain of salt because in all probability he is unsavory.

Does he pat you?

2082 What does your husband think of you? When you please him, does he pat you on the back or on the head?

Talking sense

2083 Trying to talk sense to a man is like talking to yourself. You're obviously mad in either case.

Degree

2084 Girls, a B.S. is not for thee.
Let marriage give you a Master's degree

Index